Just Beyond Tomorrow

A collection of poems and other writings
by Tony Marconi

Published by Upon My Word, Delaware, Ohio

LCCN: 2025902636
ISBN: 9798897042678

For Audrey, my cherished granddaughter:

There are no words to describe the love I have for you and the hope I hold in my heart, knowing that you will be able to see, as the poet Kahlil Gibran stated, the future. To paraphrase his words: For your soul dwells in the house of tomorrow, which I cannot visit, not even in my dreams.

With all that is sacred in me, I pray that house of tomorrow will be a home for all your joys and aspirations.

Forty-five Poems,
Four Short Stories,
and One Essay

you really ought to read

Table of Contents

Let's Catch a Cat

let's catch a cat
and ride the swing
that grandpa built
beneath the trees

let's catch a cat
and feel it purr
as trembling waves
of summer's breeze

let's catch a cat
and hear the sound
of far-off trains
and highway sighs

let's catch a cat
like long ago
when once we saw
through children's eyes

Melody

What could we know of endings
in that early season of unlocking,
when the breath of God was lilacs
whispered faint and cautious
on soft-spun breezes that seemed
to promise us everlasting dances,
too soon slowing their tempos
as autumn gently touched our limbs.

For Judi and Others Who Have Gone Before Me

when the turning comes slowly again
and somewhere we are met upon
the once-more road
the dust-whirlwind will mingle us in greeting

ages touched in granite marking pine and oak
their steady procession
know only of the moments in this day
all of us have gathered long before
and long beyond the flash when it began

Monument

Crawl back, if you will, to Lascaux,
and let the hunger of your soul
be fed with berry juice and ashes;
only be not afraid of today,
for the architects of Babel
have long since been forgiven
their crimes against Jehovah;
they have risen again to celebrate
their near conquest of heaven.
Come, then; brand your name
into my flesh of concrete and steel
and glass; let me stand as testament
to the reigning age of human wisdom.
Rejoice in the deaths of your gods
and let only now be your hearth.

For when at last this dying earth
lies hushed; and time and wind
render the land void of feature,
what then will it matter of horses
once drawn on fire-lit cavern walls?
Who will be left to grieve crumbling
stones; lofty towers and domes—
the holy cathedral and mosque,
bank and marketplace, and all
other sacred spaces once built for
the worship of unbridled hubris,
but fallen and transformed once more
by fire into sterile canvas, smooth
and clean as if no hand had ever been?

Proposed Solution
(one size fits all)

For every mass shooting:
Thoughts and prayers.
For every home destroyed
by tornadoes and hurricanes:
Thoughts and prayers.
For those afflicted by fire
and contamination from
rediscovered, buried toxins:
Thoughts and prayers.
For the underfed or the starving:
Thoughts and prayers.
For those who die from poverty:
Thoughts and prayers.
For those who live in makeshift tents,
for those who live near garbage heaps,
for those who live against walls
near train tracks, near broken shells
of buildings destroyed by bombs:
Thoughts and prayers.
Your parents died, your brother died,
your child died for lack of clean water,
for lack of basic medical treatment,
for lack of supervision while playing
in those previously sown minefields:
Thoughts and prayers,
thoughts and prayers,
thoughts and prayers…
        as if there were a caring god.

Patriotism, circa 1962

I've been here before,
marched with the Explorers
in Memorial Day parades,
holding Old Glory as the bugler
played taps, and the troop
gave the three-fingered salute.

Afterward, as the spectators
and most of the other marchers
dispersed, their duty done,
a few of us wandered, searching
until we found the very worn
headstone of the founding father,
died in 1848, and his wife four
years later. We do the math
in our heads: one hundred ten
years separate us from her.
He was only forty-nine, but she
made it to fifty-one. Next to them,
eight small stones for the children
that didn't survive, names unclear
but three barely readable dates:
one totaling but a few days, another
four years, and the oldest, thirteen.
We contemplated the unspoken fact
that we were barely older ourselves,
and we wondered at our good fortune
to be alive, with the blessings of TV
and the Top 40 to fill our soon to be
summer vacation days and nights.

Curiosity satisfied, we hiked along
the two-lane asphalt street down
to the VFW lawn where the baseball
field had been temporarily covered

by some of the rides and booths
of a small carnival that would appear
only one more time that year in our
nothing-special rural country town.
On the Fourth of July we would don
our kerchief-ties and deep green
uniforms and once again march
for the glory of the United States,
Land of the Free, Home of the Brave,
where popcorn and cotton candy
and a ride on the Ferris wheel
mattered more real than the memory
of long-dead pioneer families.

Fun With Dick and Jane

It's abandoned now, both front and side doors
secured with oversized chains and padlocks;
first-floor windows boarded with half-inch ply.
All except that one over the cement-block roof
that once covered the furnace room,
when only the bravest dared to scale it
to retrieve a poorly thrown ball or the
all too occasional textbook dropped from
the second floor by a daring seventh
or eighth grader, (though never on purpose,
or so everyone in their class would swear).

But the climb up has grown magically
shorter, and even in the bright daylight,
I am no longer afraid of pending
repercussions should a teacher—or worse,
the principal himself—spot me climbing
steadily toward a glimpse of my fading
past. At shoulder height, I can barely see
through the dirt-coated glass pane, choked air
sealed inside when, unaware to us,
time stopped here after the final third grade
class was released for the school year, never
to return in fall to add its raucous, haunting
laughter to the choir of ghosts lurking
(I suppose) in the shadows of vanished youth.
Dick and Jane, Baby Sally and Spot the dog
had once flourished in this room, though
having grown obsolete years before, would
find themselves consigned to the basement
for storage, forgotten and warped with mildew
as the world outpaced the American Dream
and became more and more lost in space.

If I listen closely, I can almost

make out the echoes, like buzzing hornets
returning to the hive now flushed and
vibrating after morning recess games.
Who cared what Mrs. Faukenstein—newly
married, and always Mrs. Frankenstein
behind her back—might have to say about
two-digit long division? There were books
hidden in the confusion of my desk;
tomes small enough to tuck behind
the scores of problems which I never
considered solving unless I was caught
while riding a flying carpet, or defending
the Alamo, or learning to tame a wild
Arabian stallion on an island.

My hand wipes the outer side of the glass
to little avail. The dust has grown
almost as thick as passing time, and I am
too weak to break the spell that all these years
and (perhaps-imagined) memories have
woven out of my longing for simple
explanations governing the course of life;
when passing to the next grade would earn us
free ice cream cones at the drug store's soda
fountain, due to the generosity of Mr. Ruzika,
the owner and arch Republican booster,
when kindness and politics were blended
as easily as childhood and the possibilities
to be found in our unbounded dreams.

Song of the Roadway Door

...three hundred miles,
        ahead the road more visible
        as the land dissolves in the pink light
                            of almost dawn

you sit beside me,
        eyes fixed and restful on my face,
        offering hot coffee from a thermos
                            while the farm news
                            breaks morning music
                            on a local station

i could be here forever,
        moving toward an unfamiliar place,
        held by speed and the vibrating engine,
        touched by the warmth
                of your breath

i could be here forever,
        even as day turns into twilight;
                you borne lightly on sheets stiffly cleaned,
                wrapping your strength within, around mine;
                prepared for tomorrow's miles

we and machines;
        only we moving, moving;
                            i could be here forever...

If I Woke to Find You

if I woke to find you
sleeping in my arms
the first light of dawn
faint against the rhythm
of your beating heart
my senses would be filled
with the taste and sound
of your breath
the scent of you
caught in shadows dissolving
as our hands entwined

if morning found you flushed
stirring beneath touches
only dreamed before
i would answer
the songline urge
with my lips
until the waiting years
fused our bodies undefined
into nerve and muscle and will
forever heard
in the echoes of your sighs

In the Crisp Sweat of Night

in the crisp sweat of night
i feel you come to me
on the distant rush of trains,
your sighs like fading engines,
floating inward and away
down endless secret tracks
toward coiled destinations

your breath fills my ear;
surges soft but urgent in the dark
i strain, try vainly to hold
thoughts as still as muscle

beyond the fields, the whistles cry,
demanding, pleading,
drawing like tendril fingers
my lips to your waiting flesh
and i feel you come to me alive,
alive in the crisp sweat of night

Chronos

we wait
    nights pass
    the stars wield slowly
    their distances
    testing the coldness of space
    for vibrations
    from the spheres
still we wait
    eternity mocks the whispers
    of pock-marked planets
    renders scars void of meaning
    stands as testament
    to the insanity
    of love set in motion by time
but we wait
    searching the zodiac
    for reassurances
    and patterned guaranties
    of courses to be steered
    through secret eddies
    until the stars are fallen
yet we wait
    content in the ebb
    of the naked moon
    knowing for this moment
    unsensed by the passing sky
    we lie as one unyielded
    before the cosmic tide

The Pause

listen, listen;
there the pause,
your breath still,
the why answered;

then soft, a motion;
your breast rises, falls,
keeping time with
the quiet in my eyes

around our bodies, the walls swirl,
screaming the frozen agony
of a world touching but not touched

farther, farther;
beyond the reach
of moments lost,
your lips part,
exhaling warm,
as my hand traces
the lines of your throat,
and feels the pulse
quicken

Prelude

tell me more
please
with each word
with every motion
I hear your breath
hear it whisper
whisper you

say the warnings
carefully
so carefully
reach them from
your hand to mine
touching only
with our thoughts

who are we now
you fearing
you whom I fear
who are we now

the threads hold
so tenuously
i dare to speak
in hush alone

There's Fire

There's fire in there, baby,
but it isn't all flame.
There's thirst flooding
from those eyes;
and o' the sticky mud
of your voice crying
for a few minutes more,
breath like hot
summer wind; fertile,
penetrating my soul.
My belly quivers
at just the thought.

You're the force unsaid, baby;
the blast phase
of a thousand million
Hiroshima bombs,
the sun in supernova,
powerful beyond
even your imagined
high-beamed lust.

You have the fear, baby,
yet only see
a reflection of yourself
in my arms.
The tremble
bidding you recoil
is but a shadow of me,
touched by your wave
and consumed.

Secret

I came to share the storm with you.
It seems fitting that amidst the violence
of pounding skies and driving waters
we should know this tension, reflected
and loosed in fireball bursts, dissolved
in the roll of collapsing thunder-waves,
resolved in our mingled gasps of delight.

We are connected by bonds much firmer
than the simple motions of our bodies.
We are united by torrents of lashing droplets
which cloak us, curtain-like, under the same
garment, making us invisible to the world
of outside judgments that seek to have us
conform to the dictates of their expectations.

And their raging, for all its noise and flashing,
can mean no more than the talk of neighbors
or the canned morality of Sunday schoolers,
straining to convince us that this enveloping
quiet we know together is but an illusion,
transient and unreal, even though the smile
on your lips bids all of nature to silence.

Notes From A Small Town

Here, where I grew up,
the roads are lazy
the air is either thick,
heavy with summer,
or sharp and crisp
like dusky fall.

Your daddy's car
smelled of old cloth,
comforting and warm
against my back,
your face framed
by the faded gray roof.

I married you
because of that back seat;
one broken rubber;
two broken lives,
and this other—
what becomes of her?

And in this endless
drifting time
of sunlight hours,
sluggishly repeated
like a mantra gone wrong,
or in the night when I am
called stranger by your eyes
and cast adrift;
I still remember
when our touches rippled,
broke the light
of a shuddering moon…

Days are formed by the drip of wood;

light melts through glass,
lies puddle on the unswept floor.
Outside, another country calls me home.

To My Love In Autumn

flame orange flares set against
yellow mint leaves
effortlessly glide in ones and twos
nestling brown into the earth

you are the burst of glory light
giving reason to the rain
giving rhyme to stalking time

winds fade to autumn's hush
whisper chill memories
the distance surrenders slowly
and crumbles into graveled roads

you are the rise of beating wings
striking high against the moon
held in flight by quick'ning breath

frost stars burst sharp and clear
on stubbled stalks exposing
the urge and fall of hill and furrow
swept toward windbreak horizons

you are the song of locking earth
tensions coiled in soil and sky
yesterdays that lie and wait
lie and wait tomorrow's sun

The Philosopher's Stone

Think, Goebbels, think: If just one almost Jew,
pinned like an insect and chloroformed by ancient history,
could snatch the fallen souls of humanity
from the pit of their collective hell,
what then will these millions so readily given in our name
contribute to the glory of the Reich?

Traitors will protest to be sure;
there are always those whose stomachs for salvation
churn fearfully at the sound of a few dying screams,
but the work must continue if we hope to be cleansed;
sanctified in the oven's scouring flame.

Tell the Fuhrer, *mein herr*, that the vermin have died;
that their ashes lie scattered on the altar of mankind.
Tell him not to fear the sight of naked bodies
piled high in sacrificial mounds;
for was not the Savior Himself naked
before their very throng
when He turned His face to Heaven
redeeming us?

Eva's Song

Twice at my hand it was nearly over,
and countless times my thoughts have let me die.
To have loved such a one as that: The world stares
fascinated, asking only to be properly appalled.

What was it like, Eva, tell, to share
your bed at his twisted whim?
Were the blood-drenched lips smooth
against your awkward body? Did he beat you down,
burn holes with cigarettes, and shave your pubis bare?

The feckless would know; they beg to know
what gives this man his power over them.
The conqueror's robe, shining,
and dropped by night at my bedroom door,
rises of its own to haunt their dreams.

These hounds of death prattle unaware;
frightened by the answer locked in the eyes
of their own silent wives.

For when, at last, the sheets have fallen free,
leaving the master of this house
prickle-pocked with cold and drained of will,
I alone am left to feel the course of history
as beads of sweat that run across my breast.

Family Album

The forties seem gray to me now:
Uniforms and long skirts; city streets in winter,
but there must have been color on Sunday.

There must have been red among the ships
and blue in the churning waters,
and vivid white through the yellow-streaked flames.
And my mother's eyes might have shone
a little greener to hear my father
speak of war with a trace of longing
for the copper sound of shells.

Those photographs of hunger seem faded now;
old stories burst time like peacocks,
breaking from their eggs.

My father hunted birds like those,
found hue and tint within their drab nests,
smelled the sweetness of their brilliant deaths.

But mother dressed those years
in gray and waited for flowers that never grew;
crayons that never came in the mail.

Father brought back the fallen sun
and freshly picked mushrooms,
then gave me to the half-blind child
whose picture he had kept.

And though she took the gift with grace,
I learned to see in her paling stare
the wish that my flesh had been canvas;
my blood a river of paint.

Speer, Upon Receiving His Calling

It crouches in the dark waiting;
I sense it breathe out,
exhaling slime thick air,
hungry for my soul

Feet of newborn legions
tramp compelling invitations
to the cleansing fires.
I pause in my room, praying
to be made golden;
hoping, for a promised honor
and an end to night's
hissing rise,
before I go all too willing
to heed the cry for space.

Banners fly their swastikas,
forcing out the weak,
erasing those vestiges
of shame cast upon our race
by hands so unworthy
that Valhalla itself wept
and swore revenge
against their mongrel world.

Fatherland, hear me:
I cannot bear to see your cities
burn red from the east,
torn like broken purses
in the traitor's hand.
Fatherland, hear me:
I step against Judah
only for my love of you.

Alone we are the starving,

the homeless, the dead.
Within your forests
and mountained farms
our quest for life
wills itself triumphant,
triumphant in its will.

Masada Cries

Masada cries,
and I am torn up the tortuous crags
of barren peaks so void of life
that even the blood
from a thousand cut throats
could never cause
a single grass blade's whisper.

Pride carries me to god-made,
man-made walls; pulls me, pleading,
to the ranks of the already fallen;
the fallen to be.

Are nations always born in death?
Is not the world a nation bound
in the sorrow of slaughter?

Yet, Masada cries,
and pride swells through my legs;
lifts my arms to shield and spear.
It whispers, a seductive harlot,
making me a man spitting
defiance against other men.

Masada stands: The rock of my soul,
the soul of my flesh; solid within,
destiny and regret, impaling
far deeper than the Roman sword.

Temple

Let the red rust run like blood
		then powder into earth again,
			and rise as Babel once more great,
				to smite the sky with steel wings
					and spit our name into the rain
that lets the red rust run like blood.

Hauntings

It was haunted. It had to be.
Old, framed like a worn wooden
artifact from ancient Greece,
but abandoned when old man
Albright put down his brushes
and stretched canvases, then died.

We all learned the story piece
by piece of how this weathering
monument to a once-promising
glory for our mostly hidden town
was built before the Civil War.
A church with few parishioners,
and fewer still after the fighting
was done and the dead were
buried in the cemetery a mile
and a half down a secondary road.

A couple of decades later,
the congregation dwindled down
to a few dozen, mostly over sixty.
A vote was taken to accept a token
sum raised by a group of younger
men who wanted a place to hold
(most shocking) dances. The belfry
removed, rumors would not be
contained: Drinking, card games,
a place where book was made
and hidden slots were available,
luring disreputable men and women
from the city on weekends. No one
was sure why they stopped coming.
Prohibition, probably, but ghosts
and imagination are more alive
in the minds of children than are

facts. So, there came a night when
a pair of unmarried lovers were
discovered murdered on the bank
of the river that flowed not twenty
yards from the side door. Now, there
was a story whispered at a campfire:
that the shuttered, abandoned place
was haunted, by a man with a hook
who used it to skewer lusting teens,
daring to neck in Daddy's Model-T,
parked anywhere in the vicinity.

And once again, the building lay
dormant, unattended for a few
dozen years until the artist bought it
for a studio. He never made much
on his work, the era of pretty children
had long since passed. Flappers
and gin and art-deco had come
to the fore. Pastels failed to provide
the necessary grit. So, he bartered
his work for food and services and then,
grown too tired, he lay down to sleep,
never to wake, but leaving a legacy
and a once-more shell of a building.

And now, grown up and returned
as a visitor to the town swallowed
by tract homes and strip malls,
I find a few recognizable streets
and familiar houses, renovated
almost beyond recognition. The old
church I attended is replaced with
a new design seemingly ready
to take flight over the rectangular brick
edifice that held the God of my childhood
firmly behind its walls, and

the dam at the forest preserve is
removed in the name of ecological
purity. Both are as vanished and forgotten
as those now-disappeared ghosts whose
preferred place of haunting has been
exorcized by plaster and new paint,
transforming the mysterious, sacred
imaginings of adolescence into
a scrubbed-up historical museum.

Requiescant in pace annorum somnia.

Evening News

We laugh behind your heads of rags
while our men prepare to shed
their blood like gasoline.

Our people die together in the sand,
clutching spilled bowels and shattered heads.
Still, the brokers cry for more.

O' powerless, powerless, hungry ghosts,
devouring honorlike substance.

Sons for sons, we've traded faiths
and proudly point to color sets
that bring the pictures of their deaths.

O' powerless, powerless, hungry ghosts,
devouring honorlike substance.

Bastion

This evening, someplace else,
soldiers die (the lucky ones).
Those less fortunate,
whose bodies lie mangled,
writhe in mud or sand,
until no longer able to scream
disbelief and pleas for mercy.

They exhale one last time
as the sheen in their eyes
fades to dull glass,
and the process of slowly
being forgotten begins.

On this side of the line, we sit
and sip coffee as we read
how the neighbor's son
has made the list.
                    More cream, dear?

The Limits of Power

This time no Messiah's voice is strong enough
to call forth Lazarus from the thick air
of his waiting tomb, for the catatonic old gent
has found comfort In the sounds of rotting flesh
and the smell of sterile rock.

"The light would hurt my eyes," the cadaver whines
to the nodding, smiling, drooling caretakers,
as they roll larger boulders to block the door.

The command softens to an invitation
then whimpers as a plea, easily ignored;
drowned out by a belch and a fart, as the corpse
rolls over to sleep his final sleep.

And outside, the Messiah hangs his head
in funeral prayer; then turning away,
smiles and moves to the next grave, shouting,
bellowing, laughing for life itself,

"Lazarus, get your ass out here, boy!
Lazarus, Lazarus…"

Gästhaus

Wooden tables rest in the embrace
of the fire's open warmth. Old men
pour wine from a bottle and sip on
memories of vintage years in pasts
now story-booked in their distant eyes.

The younger men raise their mugs in song,
preparing a chorus of frozen moments
against the maybe-hours of future age.

Whispering couples in darkened corners
steal furtive touches of reassurance,
blending with the bubbly smiles
offered by the almost-pretty barmaid
whose thick thighs tease "maybe"
beneath her short, rustling skirt.

We all have private homes, easily reached
by short walks through the snow-crisp winter air;
but to leave would be unthinkable; to leave
would be an act of wanton destruction;
for here, we are one, as a family,
kin to the forest outside to which
the falling white clings, even as we cling to
each other against the cold and empty night.

American Independence

I see you all the time on the TV.
Pesky-ass crusader, wantin' me to care.
You say the kids in Africa are hungry.
But I already know that, so who gives a fuck?
They ain't my kids; my kids are well fed
and doin' pretty good in school.
But if twenty bucks'll shut you up
and fill them empty bellies for a while,
then, here ya' go, and leave me be,
and I'll take care of me and mine.

I hear you sometimes on the radio.
Friggin' liberal tree-hugger, stealin' people's jobs.
You tell me that we're heatin' up the planet.
But maybe it's all bullshit, so who gives a fuck?
I do my part, pitchin' recycles,
and sometimes sharin' rides to work.
But if twenty bucks'll cool your jets
and make the summer days a bit less hot,
then here ya' go, and leave me be,
and I'll take care of me and mine.

I read your letters in the newspaper.
Lefty-leanin' socialist, grabbin' for our guns.
You whine about the shoot-ups at our schools,
But teachers aren't packin,' so who gives a fuck?
I've got my glock, 'n thirty round mags
for all my semi-auto needs.
But if twenty bucks will hire a cop
to protect their halls and cafeteria,
then, here ya' go, and leave me be,
and I'll take care of me and mine.

The Brilliant Monks of Golgotha

the brilliant monks of golgotha
work for the light of an afternoon
come too late into my dreams

they touch the tombstone constructed
to mark your residence and you go
singing gladly psalms of ancient times
first composed in tents

but not being musical and disdaining prayer
i find the doorway blocked
your body wedged between the stacks
still breathing but barely able to ask
which way god went

The Dismal Science

I think she was twenty-one.
when the bullet ripped through her left tit,
utterly ruining the newly purchased work suit
and forcing several department stores
to cancel her charge accounts.

And in spite of her questionable morals,
there was a slight dent made
in the pharmacy's monthly profits
when she ceased to buy birth control pills
and lubricants.

But that's the tragedy of crime for you:
Two hostile men in a big
(probably unpaid for) car,
in broad daylight, no less,
just jump out and cut down
a valuable, contributing member of society
with no regard for the consequences
and inconveniences put upon America.

God damn! Don't they know
the business of business
is business?

Founding Fathers

He owned me, not because I was less a man
than he, but by chance of birth when my mother,
raped by a former owner, bore that master
a son, increasing his wealth by forty dollars.
I was sold to the great man at the age of ten for
two hundred, as he was willing to gamble that
I might reach eighteen and maybe live to forty.

His Excellency went on to war, hailed as a hero
and given praise for his service in battle and
in the politics that followed. He was, for all
the remaining years of his life, as best I could
determine, honored by his contemporaries, and
with ever an eye to his financial well-being,
he continued to cultivate his human property.

Future generations of his unshackled admirers,
untouched by the whips of indifferent overseers
and the blows of drivers, of endless days lived in
earthen floor shacks, of unrelieved heat and cold,
of bellies never full, will ever truly comprehend
the reality of our unending labor. Our work was
forever void of personal meaning, which is itself
the truest torture of slavery. We stood condemned
even unto our posterity to an existence of unrelieved
toil sans hope of anything save bare subsistence,
until we were at last buried, vanished from memory,
our graves unmarked as if we had never been.

Yet, always, I kept my silence, dreaming, waiting,
myself a general in a one-man army, watching for
the moment the enemy's guard would be down and
my own opportunity for freedom from the tyranny
of ownership would present itself unspoken, no
voiced declaration of independence to betray my

my plan to decide the course of my own life.

And then I ran, though the odds were against me.
I had no plan or purpose other than to survive one
more day, one more meal, one more drink of water
undetected by the hunters he set upon me, that his
property would not be lost and his dignity not be
unduly impacted by the insolence of a thing less
than human in his cold and uncomprehending eyes.

And I was caught, and I was sold for a few barrels
of whiskey, placed in shackles and made to work
cutting cane in the Indies where I lived two more
years until, weakened by hunger, illness, exhaustion,
and despair, I embraced the blessing of death. And,
as I passed beyond the reach of the masters,
my last thoughts went to the legendary hero,
discussed so often by my present owners, and I
wondered if the great man would be as ready as I for
his own inevitable crossing when his time was
upon him. Would all those temporal honors that
were once and always to be his due grant him
comfort when he was reduced to the same dust as I?
And there, as his thoughts dissolved into the darkness
of eternity, would he understand that our gifts to our
mother soil were forever equal in the Creator's eyes?

Before The Nova

They were bored that night when they switched on the monitors
and discovered that the snow was in its advanced stages.
A few remaining people had left their long-since buried cars
and were leaping to their deaths from bridges.
They disappeared into the white banks below them.

A scan through each building over the next few days
confirmed the suspected: save themselves,
only a small band of militia remained alive in the world.
Plans were drawn and they waited.

On the seventh day after they had begun to monitor,
the soldiers arrived at their door, placing them under arrest.
That night they ignored the locks, withdrew their pistols,
and one by one, shot the sleeping army. Their work done,
some walked outside into the now quiet snow.
Others took pills. The last one looked into the barrel
of a gun while the trigger slid back.

> On that last day,
> the white Earth was still,
> and the Perceiver smiled.
> And the smile smelled of spring.

Scion

If I am not the son of Isaac,
why then does my almost faltering soul
fill with trembling at the discordant
shofar's demand, calling me to repent?
It lifts me into the living Breath
that blew across the void, making holy
the longing of my father's fathers
for covenant with that which is I Am.

And am I not the son of Jesu
when the drone of chanting monks resonates
midst pillar and vault, stirring within me
nascent memories of pilgrim feet,
bleeding with each step, that draw my mind
with them in awe; in amazement and fear
of the God they believed was made flesh;
of the God they prayed would make them whole?

How am I not the son of Ishmael
when the muezzin's plaintiff cry
stirs longing in the very depths of me
to see Holy Justice done on Earth
and the Peace that Allah revealed
to His Messenger come to all mankind?
Surely my heart could never be so hard
that it cannot know that God is One.

Am I not the yearning son of All,
called many names and is yet the Same?
Even as Brahma creates the world,
as Vishnu holds it in loving embrace,
and Shiva dances its cycle fulfilled,
when I close my eyes I can softly hear
the Music of the Spheres ever playing
those ancient chords that call me home again.

Helpless

Though I have every reason
to return home once again,
to seek the familiar comfort
of mornings spent watching birds
at my feeders and anticipating
the time soon to be when
the tomatoes have turned
from green to red and the yellow
squash is fully ready to be picked,
still, my mind is not quieted.

Though I have grown weary
touring cathedrals built for a faith
I do not share or castles that exist
because they have withstood
the storm-sieges of dangerous times
when rich and powerful lords
challenged each other for the right
to exploit the labor of serfs,
still, I long to perch on parapets
that once sheltered defenders
from arrow and spear and sword.

For in those moments where I float
with the scent and sound of nature
and I am, at last, at peace with the god
that comes to me on the summer air,
whose presence I carelessly allow
my being to expand and dissolve into,
the Lorelei's song calls clearly to me,
haunting, luring my spirit to return
once more to future journeys.

Rhine Cruise

See that one over there? It looks like something
out of a movie. You can almost see knights
in shining armor mounting the parapets
to do battle against a besieging foe.
Then there's another, now reduced to mere ruin,
its former defenders lost in histories
unknown to us vacationers more intent
on snapping photos for our memory books
than spending a moment more than we have to
imagining the lives of the long-since dead
men and women who sheltered behind those walls.

Then comes another and another passing
quickly as the boat cruises toward our next port.
Ten? Fifteen? Twenty? We lose count and, perhaps,
a little bit of interest as the wind
increases, and clouds block the warmth of the sun.

Besides, we say to each other, aren't all
these castles, ruins or not, simply reminders
of a shared history of irrelevant
battles and mundane political intrigues
started in the Twelfth or Thirteenth or Fourteenth
Centuries and more or less ended when Napoleon
blew most of them to hell, including the ones
the Sun King, Louis, had stripped of their treasures?

The people of those days, whether kings or queens
or archbishop electors or their servants
or soldiers or filthy half-starved, short-lived serfs
register not so much as even one new
wrinkle in anyone's cerebral cortex,
as both our touring craft and the course of time,
and the currents carrying them, roll onward
toward the same inevitable fate waiting
for each of us at our rapid journey's end.

An Evolution of Faith

And when Christ falls,
as fall he must,
and holy mosque
has turned to dust,
no prior church
of some past saint
will come to mind
or cause complaint
from those who once
made sacrifice
to Roman gods
then tossed the dice
to win the clothes
of some poor Jew
they crucified
without a clue
that on this place
one day a church
devoted to
his name would perch
and wait as time
and wind and rain
and some new god
this place would claim
for box-store or
a shopping mall
as worshippers
will heed the call
to rush to buy
some talisman-
reminder of
the holy plan
that made this site
a steady draw
for temple, mosque,
and church's wall.

Sympathy, 2017

Dear Sir or Madame,
I am sorry this response has been so late,
but I have been out of the country for several
weeks and, consequently, have missed your
pleas for my help in alleviating some of
America's most pressing problems.
Allow me to respond at this time, lest
you think I am unsympathetic to these causes.

I am home at last, and I see on the news
a photo from some other place where
a child displays his severed legs caused
by a bomb dropped on his village.
I switch the channel and am shown
images of people scavenging through
the muck and debris of dumps
where the trash of the wealthy
is piled far from their elite eyes and noses.
But, I am home, and I am grateful
not to be inhabiting such places.

Floods and fires and storm-sweep
have taken their toll among people
who remained in harm's way,
having no other place to take shelter
or the means to remove themselves
to safe locations. News stories abound
about those who survived only to return
to the nothingness that was once
their place of shelter and community.
But, I am home, and I am grateful
not to be in what's left of their shoes.

The mass shootings continue, yet
the only answer is hand-wringing;

the "ain't it awful" refrain that accompanies
thoughts and prayers offered by leaders
trying to cover their political asses until
the shock wears off and something new
and shiny grabs the public's attention.
But, I am home, and I am grateful
not to be living where the gunman was.

I know that inequality is inherent in our socio-
economic structure; that where you were born—
and to whom—will, more often than not,
determine your destiny; that successful individuals
are the exception pointed to by those who
benefit from privileges not structurally shared
throughout our unbalanced, pyramidal society.
But, I am home, and I am grateful
not to be at the bottom of the heap.

Those who can afford health care, have it,
and I am grateful to be one of those.
Those who can afford decent housing, have it,
and I am grateful to be one of those.
Those who have some reasonable measure
of future economic security, have it,
and I am grateful to be one of those.
Those whom war will never touch, have peace,
and I am grateful to be one of those.

There are rumblings against the stacked deck,
stirrings of dissatisfaction and resentment,
and a boiling anger getting ready to erupt.
Maybe the voices calling for a few more crumbs
will be heard this time, but rebellions rarely
succeed, and I am not worried for myself because
only the underprivileged will try to rise up:
Those who have everything they need, have it.
I am home, and I am grateful my life is quite secure.

Still, I want you to realize that I am not made
of stone and that your stories have touched
my heart, in part because your repeated petitions
for monetary support have reminded me
that I am fortunate enough to enjoy some
of the blessings God has chosen to grant to me
(while withholding them from others) so that
I might have the opportunity to help
my fellow man in some small way.
Please accept my check for twenty dollars.

Sincerely,

Song of the American Dinosaur

Let me tell you a tale 'bout my shiny car;
how I drove it fast, and I drove it far,
while I take you drinkin' at a swanky bar,
'cause my auto just ups my star.
My star, my star,
my star, my star,
Let's face it: I'm way 'bove par.

And you just gotta see where I'm livin' now,
where the maid works cheap, and the gard'ners bow
'cause they all got jobs (though I don't know how),
since the border's been closed for now.
For now, for now,
for now, for now.
Yes, we all feel safe for now.

So, maybe you worry that you might take ill,
but when I feel bad, I just take a pill.
And I never frown should I get a chill,
long as Medicare pays the bill.
The bill, the bill,
the bill, the bill,
And the uninsured make out wills.

O' the planet's been heatin' up awful quick,
and the CO2's getting' scary thick,
but the talk show hosts say that it's all a trick.
True or false? You can take your pick.
Your pick, your pick,
your pick, your pick,
Long as taxes don't rise a lick.

Now, it's time we started feelin' once more great,
when the gals were sweet and the men all straight,
and we were happy 'cause we knew our fate
was for us to overfill our plate.

Our plate, our plate,
our plate, our plate,
and let everyone celebrate.

Yes, celebrate,
o' celebrate,
'cause everyone pulled their weight.
Oh, yeah,
and there weren't slackers at the gate.
Oh, yeah,
and everybody could relate
Oh, yeah,
to those who didn't come here late
Oh, yeah,
and all the rest will have to wait
Oh, yeah,
to be accepted by the state
Oh, yeah,
and never with us whites debate,
Oh, yeah,
'bout correcting our historic slate.
Oh, yeah,
For Jesus made this nation great,
Oh, yeah,
which all your rhet'ric can't negate,
Oh, yeah.

So, if you try to immigrate,
and foreign ways initiate,
and with our women copulate,
and make your race a hyphenate,
then justice don't anticipate,

'cause this country's gonna work once more.
Once more, once more,
once more, once more,
this is Paradise if you're a whore.

Der Totentanz

The dream was vivid, or maybe what I saw
in the dark of night, in a cloud-covered sky,
was as real as a day with the sun eclipsed.
But the ground beneath endless cemetery plots
parted with no audible rumble nor felt quake
as those since-departed reached up and rose:
some dressed in tattered clothing,
some wearing rotting flesh,
some no more than bones,
some wisps of dust.

And I walked among them from stone to stone,
reading their names, calling an unjudged roll,
lest they be consigned to the cold anonymity
of their unmarked, unremembered forbears.

I saw a famous reverend who had often preached,
righteously, on behalf of the unborn, while nearby
rose a mother and her fetus, dead for lack of care.
They joined hands with him to form in single file
with a former president and a brutal dictator,
both of whom had prayed to the same god for power.

Along with them, worshipers of wealth, purveyors
of false witness, sycophants, and the wrathful,
those willfully ignorant, and those eternally hopeful,
each of whom had drawn their last breath believing
they would be rewarded with privilege or prestige,
as all began to march the slow step, dance macabre.

A rush of children joined in, some few well-loved,
but most dead from hunger or illness or neglect,
and more than I could count, the formerly enslaved.
Each child grasped tightly the hand before it,
each child wore a face bearing blank visage,

as if in their graves all pain had been washed away.

The line was joined by men and women of science,
those of artistic and musical fame, business prodigies,
philanthropists, intellectual geniuses, mingled with
failed entrepreneurs, those impaired in mind and soul,
those with crippling disabilities, diseases, addictions:
the forgotten, the beloved, the despised, those saved,
those damned, those forgotten forever on Earth.

I watched this ghastly parade until I realized
that I no longer could discern who was passing
before me and that the remains of the dancers
were dissolving into a barely visible trail
of shadows being carried as if on moonlight
or an unfelt breeze, though the air was still
and without the slightest roil. And I thought
a place in the line opened, the music,
like a piper's song calling for me
to take my place in the line,
but I recoiled in fear
and the gap closed.

Then, from the stars I heard laughter, soft and gentle,
and I quietly bowed my head in understanding
and acceptance that I, too, would one day, so very soon,
take my place among the dancers and step to the chords,
ever sung by God since the creation of time and space.

Reunion

I drove those miles in the fog of early light,
your voice ringing yesterday in my ears.
I saw your lips moving soft and playful,
eyes bright, melting in my mind once more.
The shapes of trees, of road signs rushing,
vaguely looming forms holding no meaning—
the hitchhiker's hurried glance passing by
in an unregistered blink; the car too full
with memories more real than the feeling
that once flooded our long-shared misty breath.
I heard the echoed sound and turned to see
those receding country roads we slowly shuffled
through summers, seasons too soon slipped
silently away and now barely heard as whispers.

When Joshua Blows the Horn

Man, when Joshua
blows the horn on your ass,
where you gonna hide?

That fucker can drown out
your dribble-mouth excuses
faster'n you can whine 'em out

I mean,
he makes cities fall
and suns stand so damn still
you can kiss
your silly tush goodbye.

Don't tell me "no," man—
I heard the cat play his pipe
over in the next county
(and the parade's comin' this way).

And getting pissed at me
ain't gonna do you no good,
'cause I ain't payin'
the silly son-of-a-bitch—
he's workin' for dimes,
and my pockets don't jingle.

Roadside Attraction

For our own safety, we are told
to stay on the recommended path
                  as up we go now,
                  through the last forest,
                  preserved museum-like
                  in this manufactured
                  moment of awareness.

The first stop:
        We see our hero
        (folks around here
        call him Lindy)
        as he stomps through
        the almost dried riverbed,
        pickaxe in hand,
        slamming at rocks.

We've blinked our eyes
        and now stand
        on a wooden bridge
        where a metal plaque states
        that here (maybe) another hero,
        the lady Amelia,
        drowned or vanished
        or some such notable thing.

        Materialized from the past,
        Lindy, in a sudden rush, sweeps by,
        ripping loose the metal sign
        and flinging it with curses
        into the river
        where it stands upright,
        half buried
        in the bolder-strewn,
        cracked mud.

He stares at it defiantly and screams,
"I told the goddam bastards,
but now it's too late!"

We all agree with pride and pathos,
but dare not linger too long.
We have to hurry, hurry rush
to complete the circuit
before nightfall
if we are to arrive
at Lindy's cabin in time
to uncover the mystery
of his own disappearance.
Legend has it connected
to Amelia somehow,
but now we are here
to see for ourselves.

We watch breathlessly
as he prepares his final meal,
his officially recorded Last Supper,
only with crackers and coffee.
The air is tense with anticipation;
heavy with the sad knowledge
that the knight has failed.
Yet, immortality awaits
as he washes the plate and cup
and straightens the room.

We strain—
for what?
Will the dead Amelia
come to claim him
now that they both lie
vanquished by
their Herculean task?

                              Has Lindy invented
                              a special suicide
                              that will redeem us?

          Or is a foulness

                              about to be practiced
                              by governmental leaders?
                              Murder?
                              Abduction?

We pray for such an answer.
Anything—
anything—
anything
but the one possibility
we want most to deny:
                              That the mystery
                              is bound up
                              in our own apathy.

And then it happens
(we think).
                    Lindy sits upright,
                    his face tear-streaked
                    from the pain of a battle
                    too dear to lose
                              but ended in defeat.

Our attention is riveted,
straining on that face.
                    We know this is it;
                    this is how it happens.

          And the lights grow dim and fade,
          leaving the room pitch in its darkness;
          somehow devoid of human life.

Night has crept in quietly,
And we notice that the guide
has left us to our own devices;
to stumble and grope
our way toward
the place where
we hope we left
the uncertain bus.

And no one is sure
if there will be another tour,
but we think not,
and we weep in terror.

Where Once We Called This Home

Wind-swept, rolling oceans
of wheat and corn,
dried to dust,
dried to ignorance and neglect,
where once we called this home.

And on that wind came the cries,
came the pleading
for mercy,
respite, and sanctuary
here, where we called this home.

And what did we care then,
save for the price of goods,
the price of houses,
of food, of toys,
when foreign hands,
dark-skinned hands,
reached for us,
and tongues we never learned
spoke words we never heard
where once we called this home.

Like ours, their children knew
hunger and want
and night's cold,
night falls sans pity or comfort,
where once we called this home.

And as our mother died,
in fire, in storm,
we sang hymns
to the glories to yet become,
here where this land was home.

Predestination

I read over a thousand books then I was gone.
I killed many men in combat then I was gone.
I taught school for thirty years then I was gone.
I bore six children that lived then I was gone.
I carved the blocks for Khufu's tomb then I was gone.
I slew the men and women of Troy then I was gone.

I had no marker when my breath at last joined the winds,
no stone bore my name in the desperate hope that someday
a stranger might read the markings and perhaps note
that I was here, and, for just a very short span of time
I mattered to someone; anyone, if even as merely the bearer
of joy or grief, anything to make me real against the void.

I worshipped the One True God then I was gone.
I wrote volumes of history then I was gone.
I fed the starving and healed the sick then I was gone.
I wrote songs that people still sing then I was gone.
I knew only hunger and poverty and sickness, an aching belly
and the shivering cold of a violent and never-ending night.

Then I was gone and piled into plague pits and the trenches
of potter's fields or laid beneath the floors of towering cathedrals
in bronze coffins carved with my name and left forgotten save by
the curious tourist who never knew or remembered or cared
who I was or why I deserved distinction when uncountable
    others,
lying nearby, had been reduced to splintered bone fragments.

I studied the origins of space and time then I was gone.
I ruled an empire and crucified a Jew then I was gone.

I loved with passion and abandon my wife, my children,
every shade and shape and contour of my ordinary life.

I was young; I was old; my days fell like autumn leaves.
Then I was gone.

The Warning

Aaron Vesuv came fully awake with the knowledge that the volcano would erupt that day. Sitting upright in his bed, he could see the cone through the window. In the near light of false dawn, the sky glowed faintly red. Another might easily have mistaken this color for the beginning sunrise, but to Aaron it was merely confirmation of the dreadful truth that had invaded his brain as he slept.

He reached for his wife's arm, then realized she had already risen. From the kitchen below he could hear her fixing breakfast, hear his son's voice announce he would plow the back acres today. Quickly pulling on his clothes, Aaron glanced at the cone again.

The sides of the mountain cut sharply upward through the green carpet of forest that surrounded its base. Against the cloudless sky, the now dark mouth noiselessly trailed a small plume of yellow smoke which rode the wind downward to encircle the town of Phillipi with an ominous crown of sulfur.

As he descended the stairs and entered the kitchen, the conversation between his wife and son became more clear, and a frown of displeasure crossed his face. They were discussing the dwarf again; a subject that disturbed him even under normal circumstances. That they could ignore so obvious a threat as the volcano for the latest gossip of that miserable creature grated Aaron's nerves.

"But can you really be sure, Nathaniel?" his wife queried over her coffee cup.

Nathaniel raised his palm. "Mother, I swear it's true. I heard it from Benjamin last night at the inn. He was with the Mayor when it happened."

The woman clapped her hands in delight. Then, noticing Aaron standing in the doorway, she signaled for him to come forward.

"Husband, did you hear the news? The dwarf found gold in the mountain. He filed with the Mayor last night. They say he's as rich as Midas!"

Aaron stood frozen in the doorway, staring incredulously. Could it possibly be that she didn't know?

"Husband! What's the matter with you? Why are you looking at me that way?"

His voice rasped like a rusty file. "The volcano explodes today."

Nathaniel looked up from his porridge, his face all smiles. "Nonsense, Father. You've had a bad dream. Come sit down and let me tell you about the gold."

"It was no dream!" Aaron nearly roared as he strode to the door and flung it open. "Look for yourself if you think I'm the kind of fool who believes in dreams."

Still smiling, Nathaniel set down his spoon and shrugged. He walked to the door and looked at the mountain. It stood silently against a now clear sky. "But what am I supposed to see, Father?"

Aaron scowled. "The volcano was smoking this morning. It will erupt today. We must flee the island at once."

His wife threw up her hands. "Have you gone crazy, Husband? I've never heard such talk. To leave home for no reason—"

"I'm telling you the reason. Our lives are in danger here."

Nathaniel held his arm. "And I'm telling you, Father, it was only a dream."

Aaron snatched himself away angrily. "Dreams are for women! I know what I know, and if my family won't believe me, perhaps my neighbors will."

"Dear Lord in Heaven!" His wife crossed herself. "You can't go to our neighbors with such ridiculous news. They'll think you're mad. The disgrace—" She rolled her eyes. "Husband, we must face these people in church, in the market. Come, sit down. Come to your senses, I beg you." She tried to herd him toward a chair.

Aaron whirled around and pointed at her. "Silence, woman!" he demanded. "So now I'm suddenly a lunatic, to be treated this way?" He slammed his fist on the table. "I'm the master in this house, and I will be obeyed!"

She began to whimper, fighting back tears. He resisted the temptation to be moved. "Nathaniel, help your mother pack. I'll return shortly."

"But Father—"

"Don't argue with me. You're still my son. Go. Do what I say." He strode out the door and let it slam behind him. From inside he could hear his wife's weeping protests bleeding through the walls, and even as he walked toward town and his neighbor's farm he knew his family would not be ready when he returned. The world had gone mad today.

****

As he crossed through the fields of newly sprouted wheat, Aaron was struck by the intense quiet that had settled on the land. Even the birds and insects had forsaken their homes for the safety of other places. The volcano had given them warning in the night just as it had whispered in his ear.

"Go," it said, "for my children displease me. I shall destroy the fruits of their labor and those who cling to their fruits."

A sharp hiss sounded behind him, and Aaron turned to see the cone spewing a short burst of gray ash. It caught a slight breeze and began falling like fine dust on the rows of plants. The powdery storm lasted only minutes, but when it ceased, the entire ground was covered in what looked like dirty snow. Aaron trudged toward the road, and when he had crossed the fence that bordered it, looked back. All he could see in those many acres were his own footprints in the ash.

He felt no pity for the wheat. Instead, he saw the ash as a blessing, for now he was sure that Daniel would believe his prophecy. Should the neighbor accuse him of dreaming, the ruined fields would bear witness to his words. The mountain had made him its messenger and would sustain his effort to duty.

From a distance, Daniel's farm appeared much larger than it was. The ancient wood buildings sprawled up and down the slopes of two small hills as if they had grown from the ground like weeds.

He found the old man and his son, Benjamin, digging post-holes. Daniel saw him coming and gestured anxiously in greeting.

"Did you hear about the dwarf?" He could scarcely contain his excitement. "My own son was there when it happened."

Aaron scowled. "I don't care about the silly gold."

Daniel waved his hand. "No, no. This is even better than gold. Tell him, Benjamin."

Like Nathaniel, Benjamin was all smiles. "The dwarf asked the Mayor for his daughter's hand. His Lordship consented. The wedding is set for next Sunday right here in Phillipi."

"There will be no Sunday for Phillipi." Aaron cast his words like stones. He turned to Daniel. "Haven't you seen the mountain today? The volcano will explode before this evening. You must take your family and flee."

Daniel frowned. He glanced at his son, and they exchanged puzzled looks. "I've seen nothing today. What makes you think we're in danger?"

"The mountain warned me," Aaron confided. "Come and see the fields near my home. They're covered with ash."

"There's too much work to take time for a walk. I'll trust your word that the fields are ruined, but that still doesn't mean the volcano will erupt."

"Such things have happened before," Benjamin agreed. "It's fortunate that there's still time to replant the crops."

Aaron's anger boiled over. "Fools!" he shouted. "Can't you understand there won't be a crop for the island this year? When the volcano—"

"Hold!" Daniel snapped back. "You sound like a frightened fishmonger in the market. Go home, neighbor. You need rest. The mountain won't harm us."

Aaron shook his head. "When the church bells ring out the danger, you'll understand. I hope you'll move more hastily then."

"And why should the church bells sound today?" Benjamin snickered.

"Because I'm going to town to warn them."

Daniel looked at his son and shrugged. He turned back to his post-hole, and when he looked up again Aaron was far down the road.

****

Before he reached Phillipi, the mountain spoke to him again. He had just come around a bend that overlooked the whitewashed houses of the town when the earth trembled beneath his feet so violently that he lost his balance and toppled into the dust. The tremor passed quickly, but as he rose, the cone began to glow as a thread of liquid fire escaped over its edge and spilled down the slope. Flame leaped up from the thread and seemed, for a moment, to take the shape of a finger pointing in his direction.

Aaron began to run toward the buildings below. There was so little time, and the volcano had made his mission undeniably clear. Daniel may have laughed at him, but the others in town would know better. That he had been chosen to save them was now beyond question.

****

The fishermen had already returned with their morning catch. It would be a while yet before the streets became crowded with customers, making the market noisy and bustling. A few of the merchants gathered at the stall of Joseph, the wine-seller, exchanging information while they drank. Aaron, dirty and out of breath, came stumbling toward them.

One of the men raised his glass in greeting. "Here now! I see the farmers have taken to early tipping. Or is it still a celebration from last night?"

The others laughed.

"Hey, Vesuv," Joseph called. "Let me give you some news to bring to your wife."

Aaron leaned against the table, panting. He knit his brows to indicate curiosity.

Joseph leaned forward. "It's about the dwarf. He's been appointed governor of the island. He's going to make Phillipi the new capital."

Aaron, eyes wide in astonishment, could barely force out the words.

"Damn the dwarf," he muttered inaudibly as his face grew

red. His breath suddenly returned. "God damn the dwarf!" he screamed.

The fishermen turned on him angrily.

"What's the matter with you, farmer?" one demanded.

"Aye," put in another. "What gives you a taste of the almighty?"

Aaron ignored the hostility. "I've come to warn you. The volcano will erupt today. Haven't you felt the earth shaking?"

"I haven't felt anything," said Joseph. "When did it happen?"

"Just a few moments ago. The cone was spewing flames. Earlier today it covered the fields near my home in ash. These are warnings to leave the island."

A sprinkle of laughter rose among the men. Joseph held out a cup. "Here, Vesuv. Although I'm not sure you haven't had enough already."

More laughter.

Joseph grinned and gestured to the offering. "Go ahead, drink. Forget this talk of eruptions and ashes. A toast to our new governor— the dwarf."

The others raised their mugs. "The dwarf!" they echoed.

Aaron swept his fist out violently and struck the cup from the merchant's hand. "Listen to me," he shouted. "The mountain—"

One of the men grabbed his shoulder and spun him around. "Shut up," he snarled, his breath heavy with wine. "Just who do ya think ya are, acting like that to Joseph?"

Aaron pushed him backward. "You're drunk," he roared. He looked at the others. "I swear I'm telling the truth. The eruption will destroy Phillipi. We must— "

Again, he was interrupted as the man lurched forward, grabbing at his shirt. "If the dwarf was here," he slurred, "he'd flatten ya. So, I'm gonna do it for him."

Aaron's open palm flew into his attacker's face, and he shoved him backwards. The man reeled into the stall, knocking over jars and spilling wine. Joseph yelled, "The farmer's gone crazy. Someone get the police."

Hands snatched at Aaron, trying to pin him down, but he twisted free and darted through an alley. He could hear the sounds of running feet as he leapt a fence and crouched for protection. The pursuers passed, and he closed his eyes in relief.

"What went wrong?" he wondered. "Yesterday I had no mission, but I wasn't crazy either."

He looked up and started. A woman he had never seen before stood staring at him. He realized that he must have taken refuge in her garden, but for the moment he was too surprised by her lack of familiarity to consider his position as intruder.

The woman gestured to the fence. "Why are they chasing you?"

Aaron frowned in confusion. "I'm not sure. It all happened so quickly. I tried to warn them about the volcano, and someone started a fight."

"The volcano?" Her eyes widened. "What about it?"

"It's going to explode today." He was suddenly excited again. "I've got to warn the others."

The woman smiled. "I think," she said, and her words calmed him, "you had better come inside for a while first."

Aaron nodded and followed her into the house. The room they entered was furnished with large chairs and an ornately carved wooden bed. The sun steamed in through the open doors, creating the illusion that the interior extended into the garden. She motioned him to a seat.

"Would you like something to drink?"

"No, thank you," he shook his head. "Who are you?"

She laughed lightly. "I should ask you the same question but never mind. My name is Lydia."

Aaron's mouth dropped open. Of course he hadn't recognized her. She never went out in public. This was the courtesan.

Lydia saw his expression and laughed again. "You just realized who I am, did you? Well, see, I'm the same as everyone else in spite of what you may have heard."

Aaron stammered. "I've heard nothing."

She pushed her hair back from the side of her face. "You're a terrible liar."

He nodded. "I don't lie."

"I can tell that. So, what's all this about an eruption?"

"It's the last day for Phillipi. The volcano is going to explode."

"How do you know?"

Aaron stood up and began to pace. "I just know. The mountain warned me last night. Today I've seen signs in the fields and on the roads. I tried to tell people, but no one would believe me."

"I believe you."

He turned to look at her, to see if she was jesting.

"You don't lie," she stated simply.

Tears of relief welled up in his eyes. At last, he had convinced another. Maybe the town would listen to the two of them. The feeling of hope died almost instantly. Who would take the word of a courtesan?

"What are you going to do?" Lydia was looking into his face.

"I don't know," he admitted. "If I could empty the town, get them to leave..."

"The dwarf could."

It was like a blow to the head. "What?"

"The dwarf could evacuate the town. All he'd have to do is ask them to go."

Aaron fought against his anger, trying to see her point. She was sincere, he thought. She really did feel the dwarf could help. And maybe he could. Maybe if...

"But how can we convince him?"

Lydia smiled. "That will be easy."

Aaron frowned, uncomprehending.

"Silly man. Don't you see? I'm the dwarf's woman." She said it with pride.

His surprise gave way quickly to excitement. Of course! All she had to do was tell him. He'd believe his own mistress.

"Can we get to him now?" Aaron was almost outside the door.

She touched his arm gently. "Wait. Not now. We can't go to him yet."

"But—"

"Don't worry. He always comes to me at noon. We'll wait for

him until then."

Aaron turned to face her, wanting to object to such a delay. Suddenly, she was pressing close, holding her body against his. He started to push away, but her smell was intoxicating. His hands seemed to act on their own, exploring her form, uncontrollable desire surging through his mind. He could feel her tugging him toward the bed, feel their clothes falling to the floor. The room spun dizzily as he drove himself into her. He could no longer see shapes; only swirling patches of color that flashed brightly with each thrust. He could hear a scream that he knew was coming from his own throat; then the world disappeared.

****

Aaron heard the rumbling from somewhere far above him. Slowly he fought his way into consciousness and opened his eyes. Lydia was lying beside him, stroking his head. He felt very heavy, more tired than he ever had before. Then he realized the room was dark, and the noise was getting louder.

"What time is it?" He tried to turn, but she held him firmly.

"Shhh," she whispered. "Go back to sleep."

"What time is it?" he demanded again.

She smiled. "It's late afternoon. Don't worry. Rest for now."

"But the dwarf," he protested. "We've got to tell the dwarf before it's too late."

She looked at him sadly, her voice a whispered monotone. "The dwarf is dead."

Aaron tried to speak, but only a harsh croak escaped his lips.

"He died in this bed last night," she explained.

Sounds like intense thunder ripped through the sky. Ash fell thickly in the garden and began to drift into the room.

Aaron knew he must leave quickly but lacked the strength to move. He would take Lydia's advice and rest first. Her hands were cool and soothing as he drifted back into sleep. When he woke, they would flee Phillipi together.

1 SEP 14

It was shortly after three a.m. that the Hauser struck ice and began taking water. The tip of the berg emerged suddenly from darkness, gliding past the bridge like some prehistoric beast snatching for its prey. The Hauser swung frantically to the starboard, clearing the monster by mere yards. For a moment the ship was quiet then a slight, almost imperceptible quiver shook her as an icy claw grazed the bow. Some of the younger officers smiled in relief. They turned to the captain, expecting a nod of reassurance; instead found his face solid and gray.

"The hull's been ruptured," he spoke to the mate, but everyone heard him. "Mr. McDunn, I want a full damage report."

"Aye, sir." He stepped to the intercom on the rear wall and selected a channel. "Who's on the Marconi?"

Someone checked a clipboard roster. "Chasek, sir."

He punched the button. "Chasek, this is the captain. Locate all nearby traffic and plot probable ERT's. Code 100. I repeat; Code 100. We're open below water."

He turned back to the observation post. From this place, high above the sea, the ship seemed calm. She rolled comfortably in the waves, reconciled once more with her spiteful lover. The captain drew a deep breath and exhaled slowly, listening to the sound the air made as it escaped his lips. Perhaps there was nothing to worry about after all. The Hauser was a lady with dignity, too proud to complain about minor injuries. If there were any pain from the wound in her belly, she had given no sign.

"Cap'n Deinoch?" He hadn't noticed the navigator's approach, and the sound of a human voice was suddenly very strange. "Should we prepare the lifeboats?"

"For what, Mr. Gibraldi? This isn't the Titanic, now is it?"

"Well, sir..."

"Well, what?" Deinoch snapped. "This isn't the goddam Titanic."

"No, sir. I guess not." He turned to go, and the captain sighed. "Very well, Mr. Gibraldi. I suppose it won't hurt to stand by. Just make sure the passengers aren't disturbed. The last thing we need right now is a panic."

The navigator frowned. "But Cap'n, those people are gonna need a lot of time. Even normal folks'd be pressed to get clear once the lower decks start fillin'."

Deinoch's jaw visibly tightened. "Mr. Gibraldi, don't question my orders." He glowered until the navigator retreated through the cabin door with a quiet, "Aye, sir."

There was a sputter from the intercom, followed by the shouting of Chief Engineer Lighthall. "Damage report; damage report," the voice rattled. "Eight sections ruptured. First through fourth filling fast. Two men missing. Pumps can't handle it. Acknowledge, bridge." Deinoch pushed the response button. "Mr. Lighthall, order full stop, then report."

Christ, he thought. Eight of sixteen sections. Then there was no hope for the Hauser; only the chance to maybe buy some time.

The intercom crackled. "Slowing to full stop, sir."

"Switch to auxiliary generators and keep full power to the pumps. How much time before the forward boilers flood?"

"Not much, sir. Maybe forty minutes, maybe less. Series five, seven, and eight on line. I can fire six up to max and get ready to blow off five right now." The engineer was nearly back to normal, reassured by his contact with the bridge. "We got lucky with the watertight doors. Slammed shut the minute we were breached. I think Evans and Deloatch were in number three when they closed."

Deinoch grunted to himself. No matter. A couple of oilers were hardly a priority at this point. He glanced at the binnacle and muttered an oath. Seven-degree list to starboard. Seven degrees in less than ten minutes! The Hauser wouldn't last another thirty. He stared at the intercom, hesitating just a moment before issuing the next order.

"Mr. Lighthall, send all non-essential engineering personnel to the boat deck at once. They are to alert the crew on E deck only in areas adjacent to the flooding. Is that clear, Mr. Lighthall? No passengers will be notified until I give the word."

"Yes, sir."

"Good. I want firemen and supervisory personnel to remain below. Dump the forward boilers before they flood, but remember, we'll need power for the lower decks to evacuate. Use your discretion as to when to switch to the aft."

Lighthall barked a short laugh. "I'm in number four and the water's up to my shins. I'll give you 'till it hits the family jewels."

A small red bulb lit up, indicating the Marconi room had information.

"Chasek?"

"Right, skipper. Nearest ship's the Normandy; estimated rendezvous, two and a half hours. I used the dead reckoning coordinates from the last watch, but maybe a rocket would help 'em out. We'd be visible in another ninety minutes."

"Very well, Chasek. Keep sending the distress. And see if you can raise anyone closer than the Normandy."

"Okay, skipper." But he didn't sound enthusiastic.

Deinoch frowned. Couldn't really blame him. The boy knew—hell, the whole crew knew—no other line traveled this far north. Only Brideway, Inc., skimmed a dollar that close. Company officials boasted they could cut travel time by three days on a round-trip crossing. What they never mentioned was the high rate of tension disorders among officers who made these runs on a regular basis. Breakdowns were becoming more frequent, and experienced seamen often refused berth on a Brideway vessel. It got on a man's nerves to be constantly watching for ice.

And this time there were the passengers. The run would have been bad at any rate—they always were—but with them aboard it was impossible. God, he could choke the idiot who thought up this one! With increasing criticism coming from the union over potential hazards, the executive board responded by staging a publicity cruise. A friggin' ship full of the physically handicapped. Cut rates for gimps, handled, of course, by the right P.R. No mention of unions; certainly nothing about danger. Just a normal trip for vacationing rehabs. Crips are people too and all that. And if a cripple could make the crossing, what would an able-bodied crewman have to bitch about?

It made no sense, but that was precisely why it would work.

Or should have. Only the Hauser had struck a berg miles from the nearest help, and she would sink, passageways clogged with wheelchairs and twisted bodies; good seamen drowning with the rest. And he, as captain, was expected to go down without a protest. Deinoch clenched his fist, trying to control the anger that was beginning to knot his stomach.

"Obligations," they had told him when he balked at this assignment. "You have obligations to your ship and her passengers. There is no room for personal prejudice aboard the Hauser."

Prejudice! he almost spat. Was it prejudice to recognize the difference between a man who could fend for himself and one who could not?

Across the room Larisch and Brown were hard at work on the maps. Final position had to be recorded in the log, and he knew that the junior officers would follow their orders to the letter. That was the kind of men they were: trustworthy, capable. A sudden rush of pride swept through him, and, just as suddenly, the feeling was replaced by shame. He was letting them down. Larisch and Brown, McDunn, Gibraldi—every sailor on board. It was monstrous they should die for a bunch of invalids, but at least he could give them the chance to fight for their lives. He owed them that.

"Mr. Larisch," Deinoch's voice was cold, demanding.

The officer looked up. "Sir?"

"Take the key to the arms locker and secure six handguns. I want you to report directly to me on the boat deck in five minutes. Under no circumstances are weapons to be distributed. Is that clear?"

"Yes, sir."

"In other words, Mr. Larisch, if anyone tries to stop you, or even so much as gets in your way, shoot him."

The young man hesitated. "Captain, sir?"

Deinoch glared at him. "Didn't you understand me, sailor?"

"Yes, sir." Larisch stiffened. "It's just that the ship's listing pretty bad. A lot of passengers'll be coming up on deck. What should I tell 'em?"

"You'll tell them to get out of your way. Same goes for the crew. If they want to argue, let your weapon talk."

"But, sir, surely the passengers---"

"That goes especially for the passengers!" Deinoch roared. "Now get moving, Mister. You've got five minutes."

Larisch snapped to. "Yes, sir!" And he was out the door.

"Captain." The intercom came on.

"Captain here."

"This is McDunn. I can't get below E deck from the bow. Water's to the lower hatchway, and it's startin' up the stairs. Same condition midship. Pumps ain't doin' much good. A lot of yellin' comin' from the cabins on E, and some of the stewards're startin' to move people into the passageways. D deck's crawlin' with gimps."

Deinoch swore. "Alright, Mac, get out of there. Hit crew quarters on your way up and give the alarm. Tell them not to waste time; I need 'em on the boats."

"Gotcha, Cap. Want I should start the stewards movin' that way, too?"

"Negative. Just get to the crew." He took his hand from the button then depressed it again. "Mac?"

"Yo."

"Use the aft stairway on B deck when you come up. Don't waste time."

"Right, Cap. See you topside."

Maybe, Deinoch thought as he switched off. He turned to the remaining officer.

"Mr. Brown, have you determined our position yet?"

"Almost, skipper," he replied without looking up.

Deinoch studied the man. He seemed strangely unconcerned about anything beyond the charts. If the orders to Larisch had had any effect on him, he was certainly giving no sign. "How much longer, Mr. Brown?"

"I'm doing the math now."

The captain pursed his lips. "Belay that a minute. I want to talk with you."

Brown put down his pencil and straightened up. "What'cha

need, skipper?"

Deinoch folded his arms. "You heard my instructions to Mr. Larisch?"

"Yes, sir."

"You understood them? What they meant?"

Brown sighed. "We're goin' down pretty quick. That's obvious. I figure less than an hour."

"Try twenty minutes."

The junior officer paled for a moment. "Then it's pretty desperate."

"Very desperate, Mr. Brown. Given the nature of the passengers we're carrying, we could lose all hands."

The younger man's face hardened. "I see, sir."

"Do you, Mr. Brown?" Deinoch unfolded his arms and paced a few steps. "I have a choice to make, and I have to make it now. Either I try to get the crips from below and into the boats, or I let every man go for himself. If I do that, some of us might live. Otherwise—" He shrugged.

Brown pushed his cap back and scratched the side of his head. "You sure of the time, skipper?"

"I will be once I've checked back with Lighthall."

"And if he confirms it?"

Deinoch frowned. "Then I'm going to order you to seal both the forward and aft gates on B deck. We can't allow passengers on deck. A riot at the boats could destroy us all."

There was no sign of emotion on the junior officer's face. He nodded and said, "I guess you'd better raise Lighthall."

Deinoch hit the intercom. "Lighthall, this is the captain."

There was no response.

"Engineering, answer."

The box crackled, went dead, then crackled again. An earsplitting whistle burst through, followed by a barely audible voice.

"Lighthall here, Captain."

"What the hell is that racket?" Deinoch demanded.

"Pop-off valve, sir." Lighthall was nearly screaming to be heard. "Steam's backed into the reserve domes on half the line.

We can dump four of the mothers out the blow downs, but the blessed valve's stuck on the fifth."

"Where's the water?"

"When I closed off section four it was near waist deep. We're up to our ankles here, but the pumps're losin' ground. Won't matter much though if we can't cool the tanks. Water temp's below freezing, and these babies'll blast sky high."

"How much time?"

"Ten, fifteen minutes."

"Lighthall, get your ass out of there now. Clear out. Head for the boats. Tell the others." He didn't wait for an answer before switching off.

Brown started toward the door. "Looks like you were wrong, skipper."

Deinoch turned to face him. "Wrong?"

"Uh-huh," the junior officer smirked. "You don't have any choice at all." The smirk changed to a grim smile. "I guess you want the forward stairs closed first."

"That is correct, Mr. Brown. Carry on." He watched the young man go.

And now, he thought, I'm a murderer. For some reason the idea didn't bother him.

Before leaving the bridge, he pulled a bullhorn and one of the spare lifejackets from the utility locker, hastily donning the latter as he made for the stairs. Outside, the air was cold, a slight wind swirling occasional flecks of snow that melted softly on his face.

Muttering sounds spilled from the half-flight above, and as he cleared the steps it was immediately evident that the boat deck was in disorder. Fifty or sixty men stood clustered in small groups at several of the launches while dozens of others wandered aimlessly around the tilted promenade. Number twelve's davits were already empty, but from the swearing of the men at the rail it seemed unlikely that anyone had got off safely. Without proper direction, an inexperienced hand could easily lose control of the ropes, dumping occupants and capsizing the boat. Deinoch growled. Gibraldi should have been more organized than this.

He scanned the crowd and spotted the navigator near the

tank rooms, dashing from port to starboard, gesturing wildly to anyone who mounted the deck. He was being largely ignored, and while there were yet no signs of outright disobedience, Deinoch knew it would not take long for stronger personalities to assert themselves. Larisch had better have made it.

He found the junior officer huddled against the central smokestack, clutching the folds of his oversized coat at the neck and waist.

"Captain!" He almost shouted as Deinoch approached him. Relief flooded his eyes.

"Lower your voice, Mr. Larisch."

"Yes, sir."

"You completed your, uh—task?"

Nod.

"Good. Now follow me."

They wove their way across the promenade, reaching Gibraldi just as he finished barking another misunderstood order to the men at number seven. Deinoch signaled him into the shadow of the tank room.

"Mister Gibraldi," he said as the navigator joined them, "the situation is most serious."

The navigator blinked. "Well, Captain, I'll admit it's a bit of a mess, but—"

"Shut up, damn you," Deinoch hissed. "There's no time for any crap. Larisch, how many pistols did you bring?"

"Pistols?" The navigator stared incredulously.

Deinoch clenched his teeth. "I told you we had trouble. It's that bad, Mr. Gibraldi. It's really that bad. How many, Larisch?"

"Six, like you said, sir."

"Okay. Give me two and some ammo. Give Mr. Gibraldi one and keep one for yourself."

Larisch did as he was told. "What about the other two, sir?"

"Wait by the main stairwell. If and when Brown or McDunn come up, extend my compliments."

Larisch moved off. Gibraldi stood, fingering the weapon uncertainly.

"Put that out of sight," Deinoch ordered. "Get back to your

post and stand by. I'll take over in a minute."

The navigator nodded dully, stuffed the gun into his pocket then wandered back toward number seven. Deinoch stepped out of the shadow, looking for high ground. The best place, he knew, would be the roof of the officer's quarters where the Englehardt collapsible boats were stored. From halfway across the deck he could see that one of the collapsibles had already been stripped of its lashings. A lone figure struggled to shift the gunwale forward; a potentially dangerous act that could result in the men below being crushed if the boat fell unguided from the footings.

Deinoch broke into a near run, raising the bullhorn as he reached the ladder. "Ahoy, mate," the metallic voice burst the semi-darkness like a shell. "Clear the roof."

Crew in the immediate area turned as they recognized the speaker.

"The old man." He could hear the tension as they nudged each other.

The figure above had also identified him. "The hell I will, Cap'n." He moved to block the ladder.

Deinoch juggled the horn as he grabbed for the rungs. "You're gonna need help with the boat," he offered as he climbed. "It's too heavy to lift yourself."

The man weighed the offer for a few seconds, then stepped aside as Deinoch pulled up.

Thanks, Cap'n," he mumbled, pointing to the rail. "Can't quite clear it."

His face was dripping sweat, but Deinoch realized it was more from fear than labor. He set the bullhorn to the side and indicated a place on the roof.

"Stand over there and get ready to heave."

The sailor turned, not seeing the captain's hand go into his pocket.

Deinoch swung his arm in a smooth, heavy arc, nearly loosing grip on the pistol as it made contact, sending the man reeling against the Englehardt's upturned keel. He crumpled and lay unmoving, his body half supported by the boat. Deinoch turned away and lifted the bullhorn.

"Attention," he called to the deck below. "Attention. This is the captain speaking."

The mulling stopped, replaced by a tense silence. He cleared his throat and continued. "Men, the situation is grave. We must move quickly now; in haste, but not in panic. Go to the nearest boat and prepare to lower. Senior crew will supervise launchings but leave no more than two men per fall. If a winch jams, don't waste any effort. Cut the lines and jump for it. There's time left, but not a lot; so, let's move out."

They had barely begun to break when he heard Gibraldi's voice bellowing from mid-deck.

"Captain Deinoch, what about the passengers? We can't just leave 'em."

Some of the men paused in confusion.

Deinoch lifted the horn. "Mr. Gibraldi, where are you?"

"Here, sir." The navigator had climbed to the tank top, where he stood, slightly elevated behind an air funnel. He raised his arms. "Captain, we've got to try to save some of 'em. They haven't got a prayer on their own."

Deinoch gritted his teeth. "Get to a boat, Mr. Gibraldi. Now. That's an order."

The navigator persisted. "God damn it, Captain. We've got to try."

His tone was suddenly forceful, rising above the clamor around him. More heads turned, riveted by the force of his words, and someone below shouted, "Maybe he's right, sir."

A few other assents rose from the crowd. Deinoch fairly screamed into the horn.

"Gibraldi, you mutinous son of a bitch. Don't you dare disobey me." He reached into his pocket, estimating the distance the bullet would have to travel.

Gibraldi remained firm. "You're not God Almighty," he thundered. "You can't order us to let those people drown." He turned his appeal to the men. "We've got to pull together now. There's no room for cowardice here." He motioned to the group directly beneath him. "Get to B-deck and start helping the stewards carry 'em up. You there," he pointed to the crew at number seven. "Give 'em a hand. The rest of you, too. No one gets into a boat without a passenger."

From where he stood on the roof of the officer's quarters, Deinoch carefully drew a bead on the navigator's upper torso. He noticed the slight surge of men toward the stairway, crowding Larisch, and he hoped the junior officer was ready. He caught his breath, then fired, heard the ricochet off the funnel, and fired again.

Even as he pulled the trigger he felt the deck tremble, then lurch as a burst of yellow flame exploded from the central smokestack. The Hauser's bow visibly dipped, and Deinoch threw himself flat to avoid being toppled from the roof. From somewhere below he could hear a muffled rumbling that built rapidly to a crescendo as it rose to meet him through the bulkheads.

He groped for a handhold, found only the cold rush of air, darkness spinning web-like among the orange-white stars swinging crazily through his mind; backward, backward...

Salt flooded his throat; thick lumps of brine that poured into him like countless piercing ice knives. He could feel the slow-motion thrashing of his arms and legs as he struck out against the choking ink, but the downward pull barely slowed. His brain seemed to expand outward, pressing his skull until his eyes bulged; and still he sank deeper, horribly deeper, his eardrums bursting as he screamed voicelessly for God in His mercy to let him die, to let the excruciating pain render him unconscious.

Instead, he began to rise. Up, up again, bobbing like a cork float on some fisherman's line. Frozen air gushed into his lungs, stabbed through the gaping holes in his ears, making him thrash wildly. His fists pummeled the water and struck something solid.

The Englehardt! He knew what it was — what it had to be — even in that moment his hand made contact, and he reached for the gunwale. He twisted and pulled, his head and stomach churning in opposite directions. He paused, clinging with one hand as he vomited, then grasped the side again. The boat felt wrong beneath his arms, and he couldn't make his leg clear the rail. His hands clawed the rib work, seeking holds in the turning mass of wood, scarcely dragging his body over the edge before collapsing under him.

Lifetimes passed. The spin in his head subsided, oh so slowly subsided, and he could almost move again. Deinoch worked his head and chest upward, propping himself against the rail. Through the icy film covering his lashes he could make out the twisted form of the Hauser a hundred or so yards off. White thunderbolts belched from her midsection as the propellers arched steadily skyward. She paused, a pillar of flame that suddenly vanished below the sea.

Gone. Just like that; not even a trace of suction to mark where she had disappeared. Deinoch stared vacantly across the waves. His vision was blurred, and he could no longer detect high-pitched sounds, but somewhere out there, just beyond his reach, the water would be full of men. Drowning men. Freezing men. Struggling and screaming men, filling the night with their terrible cries.

He twisted stiffly and groped along the boat's bottom. No oar. How could he help them without an oar? He tried to shout, let them know he was there, close enough to swim to, but his lungs were too creased with cold, too burned by salt to sound more than a wheezing cough that left him gasping for air.

Deinoch flopped weakly onto his back, wincing as something hard jammed his hip. He gritted his teeth in recognition. The gun. The other friggin' gun. The image of that stubby barrel pressing to the roof of his mouth was suddenly irresistible. Would it still fire? Probably, but not for long. How long? How much time before the salt and ice and water ruined the simple beauty of that sliding trigger? Ten minutes? An hour? Could he last another hour? Could he hold his sanity for even one more second against the searing pain that burned like molten iron behind his eyes?

Somewhere beneath the shredded flesh that had once been eardrums, the sound of his own breath roared like an exhaust valve. It seemed to keep rhythm with the ever-slight rolling of the boat. Up, down; up, down; over and over. Up, down; up—

Deinoch started as the Englehardt suddenly tilted to the side. The gunwale dipped momentarily, bobbed, dipped again, and a hand appeared over the edge. It gripped the rail, flesh white against the wood, blue veins straining with the force of its pull. It was joined by another, this one sliding as it clawed the slippery surface searching for a hold. Then a forearm, its elbow locking in place, and a soaking mop of hair rose by trembling fractions.

He tried to move, to reach toward the rising form, but his arms could scarcely generate the force to shift his weight forward. He slumped back again and stared, mesmerized by the silent movie playing only inches away.

The second arm swung over, and now a face began to appear. High forehead, dark eyes...

Deinoch screamed. Sharp angular nose...

He screamed from his guts; pure savage rage. The face kept coming as if it hadn't heard. Thin, cracking lips...

But it had heard. And it kept coming, kept rising over the tilting side.

Deinoch screamed again, and this time he could hear the sound; a massive explosion tearing through his brain.

"Gibraldi...!"

Now the chest was visible, and a foot swung over. He was still coming. The leg, knee, thigh; coming. His hip, rotten filthy hip; coming. Deinoch's teeth clenched, his left hand jamming into the coat pocket. The effort cost him his balance, sent him toppling to the right, slamming his head against the bottom.

He jerked in agony, and Gibraldi blurred out of focus, came back again, then started to whirl. The nightmare carousel spun past him, silently gaining speed. It was getting darker, but the wheel kept increasing velocity, receding farther from him, growing into an expanded funnel. Gibraldi was getting away!

Deinoch fired. Left-handed. Through the coat. He fired and fired. And fired until the gun stopped spitting flames, and a coal black sun blew up inside him.

****

A low, thick bellowing called him slowly into consciousness. He swam dully through the fog-laden layers of dream fragments that snatched tauntingly from the dark. But the noise persisted, rumbling from somewhere outside him, demanding his attention.

Reluctantly, he came awake. The sky had turned into a thick gray, barely distinguishable from the sea in the false shades of fading night. A heavy mist curtained the air, stinging his face as a stiff wind slapped against him.

He eased himself into a sitting position, wincing at the pain that slashed through his head. Then he remembered Gibraldi, and for a moment his blood surged. But the navigator was gone; not even a trace of corpse floated alongside. Nothing, for that matter, floated alongside.

He sighed heavily in relief. The Englehardt must have drifted away from the bulk of the wreckage, though undoubtedly a fair amount would be visible once the sun had come up. He felt the deep-pitched sound again and turned. Something was out there just beyond him, a little closer than before; something very familiar, but made deformed by his ruptured ears. He peered into the half-light, squinting until his eyes hurt.

The noise came again, a bit more distinct and over to the right. Then he could see it: a small twinkle of light moving along the horizon. It was joined by another and another; a whole string of tiny candles poking through the mist, taking shape…

The Normandy!

He watched, almost afraid to hope, as the flickering lights danced nearer. If it continued on its present course, he'd be within hailing distance in another hour.

He waited.

Dawn broke slowly into light rain that reduced the ship to a dim phantom toy, barely perceptible among the rising swell of the waves. He sniffed the air. There'd be a storm before noon. A regular squall, he reckoned, but by then he'd be safely aboard. If his luck held.

It didn't.

For a brief while, the lights drifted straight toward him as if drawn by some invisible magnet. Then somewhere to the ship's port a green trail broke through the rain, glowing steadily skyward until it flared into an eerie white halo. And the Normandy stopped.

Deinoch stared in dumbfounded amazement. There were

other survivors. But how? Thrown free like himself? Jumped? But where did they find a lifeboat? No time to launch before—

Of course! Number Twelve. It had spilled overboard while Gibraldi was in charge, and some of the crew had swum for it. He almost laughed out loud. They were safe. No matter what happened now, he had been proved right. Some of the crew had made it, and he would be vindicated. Gibraldi and all his accusations could rot in Hell. He had made the right decision, and his crewmen were alive. Alive. On their own power, unhindered by a bunch of crips.

The thought gave him satisfaction, and he savored it while he waited. He was still savoring it an hour later when the Normandy changed course and began to pull away, making twenty knots to outrun the gale.

****

(Excerpt from the personal log of Edward H. Janis, Captain U.S. Merchant Marine vessel, Normandy): "1 Sep 14 ... There are some men who deny the existence of an all-powerful Agent actively intervening in human affairs. But I would put it to those doubters to ponder upon the likelihood of any one person surviving a devastation of the Hauser's magnitude without divine assistance.

"How much more miraculous, then, the rescue of those thirty-eight persons in Lifeboat #12? To be sure, a certain amount of coincidence might be attributed to the fact that this boat had already toppled free of the ship and was within the limits of reach of a normal swimmer. But when we consider that of the survivors, all but one were passengers afflicted with severe physical handicaps, the intervention of Providence seems to be the only explanation for their deliverance. And if further evidence were necessary to convince those agnostics, I would bid them to puzzle this: How was it possible that the only surviving crew member, Senior Officer Leocadio Gibraldi, whose skull had been creased by flying debris that had rendered him unconscious, was able to be plucked from the freezing water by those very same cripples who were scarce able to save themselves?

"Shortly after receiving medical attention aboard this ship,

Mr. Gibraldi regained his faculties in full and was able to give a brief description of the Hauser's rapid demise. He was badly shaken, and when I inquired as to the likelihood of other survivors, he grew somewhat agitated and stated that since no other boats had gotten away prior to the boiler explosions, there would probably be no one left to rescue. With this opinion I concurred, and given the rapid deterioration of the weather which could place this ship in harm's way, I have ordered the helmsman to resume our normal course.

"But it is with the deepest regret that I record the passing of Captain Deinoch and the crew of the Hauser. Rather than attempt eulogy or tribute, let it only be said that they have gone down with their ship. In doing this, Captain Deinoch has lived up to the highest tradition of the sea, putting his duty to his charges even above his own life. He will long be remembered for his selflessness.

"1 Sep 14 (Supplemental) ...

"I have just returned from sick bay where I visited again with Mr. Gibraldi. Of all the persons aboard the Hauser, I believe it is he for whom I feel the most sorrow. Terrible enough to have died in the cold cruel sea, as did his fellow crewmen, but mayhaps much worse to bear a lifetime of memories of that awful night.

"It was with the intention of easing his torment that I paid him this visit, and in my own clumsy way offered what sympathy I could, finally reading to him my entry concerning the fate of his Captain and ship. He lay silently as I spoke, but although he uttered no sound, I do believe there was some comfort in my words, for as I turned from his bed, I was sure I saw him smile."

Divine Encounter

It started with that damn personal ad in the classifieds. I wasn't particularly looking for anyone at the time, but I like glancing at those postings on occasion just to reassure myself that there are plenty of people in the world that might be more neurotic, or, at the very least just as lonely as I am.

Now, I consider myself somewhat adept at translating the abbreviations used to indicate the type of person placing the notice along with a qualifier as to what they are looking for. I sometimes take a bit longer when unfamiliar combinations present themselves, but I've never had anything present itself that I couldn't eventually figure out—until that day.

I had been sipping coffee at the downtown diner, saying a friendly hello to the familiar people who regularly stopped to grab a cup of Joe on their way to work. Living in a small town and being a writer meant that I could indulge myself in daily rituals that allowed me to savor the knowledge that the only deadlines I needed to meet were measured in weeks and months, and even then, were often flexible.

As I was about to close the paper and head home to my key-board, I took one last glance at the inside back page and saw it:

BBBBW GSOH ISO LTR 4 SHFI WAA

Like one of those daily puzzles that catch your attention long enough to compel you to solve them in order to feel smug about the quality of your mental faculties, this pulled me in.

"Hmm…," I thought. "Four Bs in a row. I did a mental scan of the B-words I'd identified on previous occasions, and in a few moments had my ah-ha revelation. *Big, beautiful, black bi-sexual woman."* Yup, that had to be it.

The GSOH came next, and that was so standard that it was easy. *Good Sense Of Humor*. ISO and LTR were also obvious. *In Search Of and Long-Term Relationship*. My cognitive abilities were humming along, and I was feeling ridiculously good about my ad-interpretive skill set until I focused on that last piece of the puzzle: 4 SHFI WAA.

Oh, the 4 meant just what it said. *For* a specific purpose. And the WWA was also a given. *Will Answer All.* But what the hell was SHFI? *Self Help Financial Investments? Stimulating Horny Friendly Imbiber? Steely Handyman For Intercourse?* Nothing I tried made any sense, and the more I thought about it, the more challenging it seemed.

I went home and went back to work on a freelance article I was halfway through, but I found myself constantly distracted as that acronym kept coming back to me all day long. By late afternoon, I decided that I wouldn't be satisfied until I knew, so I wrote a note and addressed it to the box number provided in the ad:

SWM ISO meaning 4 SHFI write or F2F

I had no sooner e-mailed the newspaper with my order than the phone rang.

A husky, but very feminine voice said, "Is this the single, white male in search of the meaning for SHFI in my personal?"

I was too stunned to respond.

"I know, I know," the voice continued. "You weren't expecting such a quick response."

I recovered my tongue. "But it hasn't run yet," was all I could muster.

"What difference does that make? Are you or are you not interested in *saving humanity from itself*?"

I want to point out that I have never claimed to be divinely inspired, but it suddenly dawned on me that my caller had just supplied me with the meaning of SHFI.

"Are you serious?" I asked. "Your ad was about looking for some volunteer to go crusading to stop people from destroying themselves?"

"Of course, I'm serious. I've got too much to do running the universe to go playing practical jokes."

For some reason, I felt defensive. Maybe it was her tone. Or maybe I was more than a little freaked out by the circumstances, by the timing of her call.

"Who the hell is this?" I demanded.

She laughed. "Nobody. Not from hell, anyway. You've got the wrong place."

I was taken aback. "What are you saying? Are you claiming to be— "

"Your Heavenly Mother? The Spirit of Life? The Lord—or is it Lordess in the feminine? I'm never sure when you people veer from masculine descriptors. Not that it matters, anyway, but let's make it easy. Just call me God."

"This is crazy," I said. "God doesn't make phone calls. Nor does He, uh, She place personal ads in the paper."

"Why not? I've tried every other way to get through to your kind. Floods and plagues never worked. You quickly forget about what war and famine do. You've become adept at living in an ever-degrading environment. So, I figured, why not throw out some bait in a few sexually oriented ads."

"And that's working for you?"

"Too soon to tell. You're my first response."

My curiosity was piqued, and I decided to play along. "So, how's this thing supposed to work?"

"Well, let's meet for coffee, and I'll fill you in."

I suppressed a laugh. "God wants to meet me for coffee?"

"Sure, as long as you agree to pay, 'cause I don't carry cash on me."

"And you couldn't just make some appear out of thin air?"

"Of course I could. But I won't. Filthy lucre!" She almost spat those last two words.

"Okay," I agreed. "When and where?"

"Fifteen minutes at your favorite shop."

"And how will I know you?"

She just chuckled and hung up.

****

I wasn't sure what to expect and given that she turned out to be exactly who she said she was, I suppose she could have appeared any way she wanted. But she pretty much looked exactly like I'd pictured her, and as I stood by the counter in the coffee shop, waiting for her to arrive before I placed my order, she strode through the door as if she owned the place. Five-foot eight, around a hundred sixty pounds, forty of which was in her boobs standing firm under a thin T-shirt with a capital letter G printed across the front. The tightest short shorts I'd ever seen and legs like mortal sin! Corn rows down past her shoulders, pouting lips and epithelial eye folds that seemed emphasized within her deep chocolate face.

I tried not to stare, but I couldn't help it. She was hot!

She walked right up to me and pressed close enough so that only I could hear when she whispered, "I know you're happy to see me 'cause that sure ain't no banana in your pocket!"

I realized that I had turned red because I could feel the heat rise from my neck to my scalp.

She grinned and said, "Perfectly normal reaction for a mortal. I'd tell you to fight it, but you really won't be able to control your desires as long as you're in my presence. Let's skip the coffee and take a walk."

I was embarrassed enough to be relieved at her suggestion, and we ducked out of the shop and strolled over a couple of blocks to a residential area where well-manicured lawns replete with sculpted flower gardens bordered lots often dotted with low-hanging flowering trees. The air was comfortably warm, and a light breeze carried the fragrance of mown grass and the hum of bees.

Neither of us spoke for quite a while until I finally asked, "So what is it you want, and why do you think I can help you?"

Her voice took on the tone of wind chimes. "You won't be helping me. You'll be helping humankind. Maybe."

"By doing what?"

"Publishing something important." She must have seen the look of incredulity on my face because she quickly added, "Relax, you're only going to make the Biblical corrections. I'm going to line up authors for the Koran and the Vedas, and any other so-called holy books that people have been misquoting and misinterpreting for far too long."

I shook my head. "You expect me to rewrite the Bible?"

"Not all of it. Just part of the Old Testament."

"What about the New?"

"No need. There's only a couple of verses in there worth a damn to begin with, but it wouldn't hurt if you'd point them out once the hypocrites come after you."

I stopped dead in my tracks. "I'm going to be persecuted if I do what you're asking me to?"

She sighed. "That's usually what happens to people who try to do right by humanity. Look what they did to Jesus, and believe me, he was much more charismatic than you're ever likely to be."

"But wasn't he your son? I'd have thought you'd be upset when they nailed your own kid up."

"Of course I was upset, but he knew the risks," she paused, "and the rewards."

"Heaven?"

"Don't be silly. There's hardly enough room for just me up there. I like my privacy too much to start sharing the place with mortals."

"Then what reward?"

"Immortality."

"But you just said— "

"No, not the living-forever kind. The having-your-name-remembered-for-all-time-to-come. Well, at least until humanity goes extinct, which it inevitably will."

"Then why do you want me to help save it now?"

"Because I hate watching one of my creations destroy itself before it has to happen. Your species can get its priorities all wrong. You can spend precious time obsessed with getting high or getting laid while much of the environment is an afterthought to you."

"That's not entirely true," I objected. "A lot of us wish things were different."

She laughed. "Really? Then what was your first thought when you saw me come into the coffee shop? Getting into my pants, right?"

"Hey," I started to protest. I didn't—"

"But you were thinking about it, right?"

For the second time in her presence, I blushed.

"You knew that because you're omniscient?" I asked.

"It's because you're a healthy male," she said wryly, "and I know what men think about. Don't get too flustered. It's the way I designed you. Keeps the species going. Besides, I have that same effect on all genders whenever I'm in a corporeal state like this."

She paused, passing her hands down across her body. "Look, I advertised as a bisexual woman—although I could have just as easily been trans. M to F or F to M, no matter. But don't make the mistake of thinking gender has anything real to do with me. So, no, I didn't knock Mary up, and I'm not going to have sex with you in any foreseeable future."

I sighed. "All right let's get to it. What exactly is it that you want me to do?"

"You've decided to help me out, then?"

I shrugged. "When God calls, what else am I supposed to do?"

"No less than when another person asks for help. That was the most important message in the whole New Testament, of course. You know about the Good Samaritan, right?"

"Go thou and do likewise," I quoted.

"Bingo!"

"So, why should the Old Testament need special attention? The same message that Jesus gave in Luke's story could easily be summarized by what he said in Matthew 22:37-39 which was taken verbatim from Deuteronomy 6:5. 'And thou shalt love the LORD thy God with all thine heart, and with all thy soul, and with all thy might.'" I wondered if she thought I was showing off just because I could recite my two favorite verses in the Bible.

"Still," she said, holding up a cautionary finger, "I gave specific instructions how to do that to Moses, and he screwed it up."

I arched an eyebrow. "Are you talking about the Ten Commandments?"

"What else?"

"But almost every Christian or Jew could name them—or at least most of them—off the top of their heads."

She made a tsk, tsk sound that sounded like a tingling bell.

"But they're only partially correct." Her hands had gone to her hips, and she was watching me for a reaction.

I didn't disappoint her. My brow furrowed, my eyes narrowed, and I found myself scratching my head in an act of non-comprehension.

She gestured with her head. "Follow me."

We continued walking down the sidewalk until we saw the first one: A yard sign displaying the Decalogue. Two doors down was another one, and four more sprouted across the street before we reached the end of the block. It occurred to me that these signs were so ubiquitous that they had grown invisible to me. Yet, as I thought about it, I realized that I had been seeing them all over town for quite some time now.

She stopped in front of one and pointed.

"That!" It was an accusation.

I scanned the words. "So, what's missing?"

Her finger moved along as if she were counting the words. "Oh," she said with an undertone of sarcasm, "just the words Moses forgot after he broke the first set."

"You mean when he threw them at the Golden Calf?"

"Shattered them into a million pieces, which meant he had to go back up the mountain and carve them out again. The problem, of course, is that he was working from memory, and he left out a lot of what I originally told him. Frankly, the only thing worse he could have done was leave all the *nots* out."

"And you want the missing stuff put back in?"

"You've got it. I'm going to dictate the whole thing again, and you're going to put it on display all over the country."

"But where will I get the money for *that*?"

She snarled. "That filthy lucre again! It's always the excuse for you humans doing the wrong thing."

"Well, most of us Americans weren't born wealthy, and we have a hard enough time just earning enough income to live. And that's not even counting the rest of the world's poor, desperately struggling to survive on the limited resources available to them." I paused then realized I was getting angry. "So, whose fault is that, anyway? You're God, for crying out loud. Why don't you fix this broken planet you've created so people won't have to suffer?"

She shook her head slowly. "If I did," she answered softly, "what would make your lives mean anything?"

"I, uh, I don't...I mean—" I stuttered.

"Yes," she said and gently touched my cheek. "You see it now."

Where her fingers brushed against my skin a sense of penetrating clarity seemed to radiate upward and into my consciousness, as I understood that the only reason for humanity's existence was to be found in the definitions we gave ourselves. And equally clear was the knowledge that our defining moments were the result of the conflicts we immersed ourselves in. Without struggles to challenge us, there could be no personal meaning.

I dropped to my knees and buried my face in my hands.

"Please, God, tell me what to do."

She leaned forward and kissed my head then laughed.

"Like hell, I will. The only thing I want from you is a little editorial revising to a set of three-thousand-year-old rules. What you want to do with them from there is up to you. Billboards, skywriting, an upcoming thing called the Internet—use your imagination. They need to get national attention, but don't go using lack of money as an excuse. Okay?"

I got to my feet. "Right," was all I said.

God walked over to the yard sign and plucked it from the ground.

"You got a pen on you?" she asked.

"I'm a writer. I always have a pen on me."

"Good, then copy down my additions under the printed version and don't mind if I use modern day vernacular. This time I want everything to be crystal clear."

We sat on the curb, and she began.

> **I.** I am the Lord, thy God, and thou shall have no other God before Me *including the deity of your own ego, which you serve whenever you assume that I need you to defend Me or that you are empowered to pass judgment on your*

neighbors on My behalf.

II. Thou shall make no graven images to worship in place of Me, *including the Scriptures, Old and New—words you elevate as if they had more worth than your fellow human beings whom you dare to condemn based on your selective interpretations of arcane and archaic content.*

III. Thou shall not take My name in vain, *which you do whenever you claim to speak for me to justify your petty hatreds and bigotries toward those of My children whose differences you refuse to tolerate.*

IV. Remember to keep the Sabbath holy *and the rest of the week as well. Do not profane it with your indulgence of racism, sexism, classism, heterosexism, or any other abuse of power.*

V. Honor thy father and mother *by being yourself a dutiful parent, not just of your own children, but of the children of the world.*

VI. Thou shall not kill, *not even through indifference or inaction by allowing your fellow human beings to suffer and perish in squalor.*

VII. Thou shall not commit adultery, *neither by being indifferent to your spouse's emotional and physical needs nor by being concerned with your neighbor's sex life or orientation.*

VIII. Thou shall not steal, *not even by keeping from others a life of dignity by refusing a living wage, adequate health care coverage, and equal access to educational opportunities for them and their children.*

IX. Thou shall not bear false witness *either by clinging to half-*

truths as a justification for continuing to disenfranchise the powerless or by choosing to remain uninformed and uninvolved in order to maintain the status quo.

X. Thou shall not covet, *including the fruits of thy neighbors' labors by demanding that they be employed without adequate compensation so you may enjoy a better life-style at another person's expense.*

I finished writing then looked over at her.

"You know, nobody is going to believe I really spoke to you."

She smiled. "Some will, and that'll be a start."

I gave her an ironic smirk. "But mostly I'm the one who's going to catch all the shit, right?"

She exhaled deeply. It smelled like lilacs. "Someone has to. That's the way it works with mortals." She paused as if considering something. Then she gave me an impish grin. "You're a good man. I knew that when you took a chance on meeting me, and I know you've got some hard times ahead. So, I'm going to leave you with a touch of inspiration for you to remember whenever you start to have doubts."

I was a bit surprised. I hadn't expected anything as a reward, and I told her so.

"Oh, it's not a reward," she said. "Just a split-second moment for your personal pleasure because I like you."

"Only like? I thought God was supposed to love everyone, me included."

"Don't push it," she cautioned. "I told you we weren't having sex."

I blushed again, and she laughed again, wagging her finger at me once more.

"See, that's why you're going to succeed. You're quite persistent."

I recovered from my embarrassment. "So, if it isn't a roll in the hay, what did you have in mind?"

"How'd you like to see me for real? Well, not all of me. Just part."

"You're joking, right? If I recall the story, Moses wanted to take a good look at you, and you covered his face so he couldn't see yours. All he got was a glimpse of your ass—which I'm sure is quite beautiful, but that seems a bit far-fetched since I've been looking at your face all afternoon."

"But not my real face—which no one may ever do. And since Moses only saw me as a man, his view of my butt wasn't much of a thrill for him."

"So, you're going to let me see your female rear?"

"From your perspective, something even better." And without warning, she lifted her T-shirt up, covering her head.

Even as I gasped, her amused voice bubbled, "I didn't even have to hide my face, did I?"

Then her empty clothes lay next to me on the sidewalk.

****

It's been seventeen years now and yesterday marked the rental of our two hundred fiftieth billboard. Twenty-three of us pooling resources and believing that we might really make that difference She wanted. It seemed like the right time to publish our origin story, and hopefully it will draw more volunteers to the cause. I've endured enough of the insults and threats and the nonstop mockery from the general public to know the release of this article will only engender more of the same. I have long ago resigned myself to whatever may come because She knew I would and because of her parting gift to me.

No, not her boobs, though they were truly indescribable in their perfection. It was Her laughter, and the capricious way She told me I was loved because of who and what I was. She knew I'd never look up at her face, even if She hadn't hidden it. And if She could accept me so unconditionally, how could I do less for Her?

Let's face it: You've got to love a God like that!

Intention

He had hoped—no, prayed—that the beatings and the lashes that had already rendered him unconscious several times during the night would numb his mind so severely that the pain from the nails would be at least partially dulled. But when the iron tips drove into the flesh of his blood-streaked wrists, passing between the tendons he knew would support his weight for the hours— perhaps even the days—it would take him to die, he could hear his own screams rise involuntarily, venting an agony beyond mortal comprehension. Then, as he begged God Almighty for the mercy of a quick release that he knew would not come, the third, impaling spike rammed through his ankles momentarily inducing a semi-stupor that disoriented him as the cross was raised into place.

He hung, drifting in and out of mental focus, acutely aware of the constriction in his chest that made him gasp for air as his body involuntarily forced his legs to push his torso upward to relieve the pressure on his lungs. His movements were made all the more tortuous by a fourth nail that had been driven into the wood at a height that would catch against the base of his spine, tearing the flesh into an open wound that would become increasingly severe until his futile efforts would sufficiently weaken him so he could no longer rise, and he would, at last, suffocate.

His suffering became his whole existence, even to the degree that no other thoughts or memories could provide even a momentary distraction. He was aware that there were other condemned men on crosses spread out along the highest places on the hill. He had seen them when he had reached his own execution site, had vaguely noted that they were in various stages of dying or were already expired and being picked at by crows. He could hear some of them now, mostly moans or, at best, babblings, but occasionally came a protesting query to God as to why He had forsaken His servants.

The sun beat down on his naked body, quickly burning him into a mass of blisters even as time ceased to exist. There was only now, only thirst, only the involuntary physical reaction of writhing and the accompanying stabbing in his gut as the gases in his intestines expanded, forcing his bowels to expel streams of filth down the wooden post behind him. He tried to croak a plea for water, but he could not form the words, and he knew that there was no one there to hear him even if he were able to do so. His awareness, such as it was, went on and on and on…

In the twilight mode of his crucifixion-induced coma, Joshua's spirit prayed that his life could finally end. He hung momentarily in the limbo of that supplication when, without warning, his body spasmed with a new, searing stab of pain as he felt the slash of bone slicing through flesh, and he knew that the soldiers had broken his legs. The weight of his sagging torso pressed against his lungs with so much force that they could no longer draw even the faintest involuntary trace of air, and he realized he was undergoing the last throes of suffocation. In his final moment of barely flickering consciousness, he understood that it was finally over, and that he was glad. If this was God's will, whatever was to come was no longer in his hands.

His last exhalation came, the pain ceased, and the crows began to feed.

****

Somewhere, huddled in an obscure room, a handful of his followers tried to understand what his life meant. A few days later, Magdalene met with Cephas, the Rock, and a new chapter of Joshua's story began, though by the time a man named Paul entered the drama, no one could have seen the unprecedented religious upheaval that was coming. Except—as future Christians would argue—Jesus Himself, who was, after all, Divine and therefore omniscient.

****

He opened his eyes and was momentarily blinded by a bright light that brought a flood of tears running down his face. He lifted a hand to block the glare, discovered that it was no longer pinned against a crossbeam, and realized that he was pain free and lying propped up on some kind of bed made of a kind of cloth that was softer than anything he'd ever lain on before. As his blinking slowed, he could hear the sounds of voices, and blurred shapes began to form into human beings, one or two of whom were dabbing at the slowly subsiding stream of fluid pouring from his eyes. Someone was talking in a language he did not understand, then something that looked like a pair of shiny, hard figs were placed over the top of his head next to his ears, and he could hear another voice speaking Aramaic with a terrible accent.

"This is your life, Jesus Christ!"

There was the sound of many hands clapping, and the air was filled with strange, rhythmic, discordant music. The shapes had come into complete focus as fully formed people, and one of them—the woman who had spoken—was seated next to his propped-up cot while several others moved strange boxes—small carts of some kind—into various positions. Behind them there were people sitting as if in an amphitheater watching some kind of play in which he had somehow become one of the performers.

He tried to stand up but was held in place by leather straps at his chest, hips, and legs. The woman responded to his efforts by placing a hand on his shoulder. He recoiled at the familiarity. She smiled, removed her hand, and spoke.

"You are safe now, Joshua. We know you have a million questions for us, and we have many for you, as well. Just try to be comfortable, and everything will be explained. Are you thirsty? Would you like something to drink?"

He nodded, and someone brought in a small table on wheels with a pitcher of water and a cup that he could see through. He took a sip of the liquid and found it tasteless but nonetheless soothing.

"Where am I, and why am I bound?"

"You'll be completely released in a short while. Right now, it's important that we make sure you're totally recovered so you don't accidentally hurt yourself. You've been unconscious a very long time, and you'll require assistance to walk without stumbling."

"So, I'm not dead?"

"Oh, no; on the contrary. You are very much alive."

"Am I come to meet Elijah?"

She laughed, and her voice sounded like a tinkle of bells. It was echoed by the audience.

"I'm going to explain that now, but you will undoubtedly have a hard time understanding what I say. So let me begin by reassuring you that none of this is the work of either Adonai or Satan, and that there is no magic involved."

"Involved in what? Again, where am I?"

"Well, Joshua, it's not just where. It's when as well. You've been asleep for over two thousand years. Our best guess is that you were crucified in 3793. That's about 33 C.E. by our calendar. By the way we mark time, the year is 2256 C.E."

His eyes went wide. "So, I didn't imagine it? The Romans did try to kill me? At Passover?" He looked at her, trying to make sense of what he'd just been told, but he felt stunned. "Uh," he stammered. "It was in 3791."

She smiled. "See, that's one of those things we didn't know for sure. There are lots more, so why don't we do it this way for the sake of our studio audience and the HBO production crew when they go into editing? First I'll tell you what we know then you can ask me whatever you want. After that, I'll ask you to fill in some details, and maybe, if time permits, we can take some calls."

"Calls?"

"I'll get to that. Now, you're going to ask me to explain some of the words I am using, but try to hold off until I get done, okay?"

He nodded. "I'll try. But if I can't understand you— "

"Of course."

She shifted in her chair slightly, and he noticed that she was wearing pants like Persian men. He forced himself to get over the shock. At least her arms were covered with long sleeves.

"We know your name is Joshua Ben Joseph—"

"No! Joshua of Nazareth. I don't know who this Joseph is that you think was my father, but if you're going to start calling my mother names—"

"I wouldn't think of it. Mary is—it is Mary, isn't it?"

"Yes."

"Well, Mary is revered in this time almost as much as you are."

He tensed, his jaw tightening. Then he spat out the words.

"Revered? That's blasphemy."

"Well, see; that's why I need to explain things to you."

"Then at least get your facts straight."

"I'm trying, but part of the problem is that you've had a profound influence on the history of the world, and there are a lot of myths that have sprung up concerning the details of your life."

He frowned. "Myths? About *my* life?"

"Right. Okay, let's start by explaining that our present-day calendar is dated from the time of your birth. There is a world-wide religion called Christianity based on the premise that you were Yahweh's actual Son, and that your mother was a virgin."

For a brief moment, he couldn't make sense of her words, then the meaning of what she was trying to say leapt into his mind, and he almost snarled.

"How dare you try to speak the name of Adonai? How dare you try to claim I am some kind of demigod? Do I look like a Heracles or a Theseus?"

The woman started at his outburst but quickly regained her composure.

"No offense was meant, Joshua. We have no written records of your actual birth, and, as I said before, there are many stories that were told after you disappeared from Judea. Some of these were written down much later, and that's where the idea that Mary was the virgin wife of a man named Joseph came from."

He snorted. "Like someone would keep a wife who became pregnant with another man's child. No, I was almost three before she took up with Matthias. He wasn't too bad a man, and I was fortunate that my mother was such a wonderful woman. Kept us fed. Wouldn't let her new husband beat me when he got drunk. Took care of my siblings, too, even though they were his children, not hers. And when he was sober, he worked. Taught me how to frame houses, and he made her a table and some chairs. She made him James and Joses. A virgin! My bleeding feet!"

"So, you're saying your own father—"

"Ran out on us. Mother said he was a centurion and had to leave with his company, but I never believed he really cared for her other than to use her for his own pleasure, and we never heard from him while I was growing up. I bet that messes up that religion you were telling me about. But I don't get why it's called—what was it? Cincinatity?"

"Christianity. It's the Greek word for the Messiah. That's who they say you were—are."

"Now I really don't understand. You said you knew I was crucified. How is a condemned and executed prisoner supposed to lead the Chosen People to a victory against Rome? By the way, who's the emperor now?"

"No one. That empire fell apart about five hundred years after your death."

"My death? You said I was asleep."

"In a way, Jesus. Uh, that's the Greek for Joshua. Human beings have learned a lot of things since you used to walk the earth. We've developed a method for reproducing called cloning where we can make twins out of living things. Not too long ago, we learned how to replicate something called RNA, where a person's memories are stored. So far, it's only been used by some really rich people to extend their own lives, and it's pretty likely that's about all it would have ever amounted to if your body hadn't been discovered twenty-three years ago."

"How could my body still be around all this time?"

"It was hidden in a cave, mummified. It still wore the remains of a crown of thorns, and there was a piece of wood with 'King of Jews' scratched on it in Latin."

Joshua lowered his head. "Yes," he said softly. "They mocked me."

"But that made identification of your body possible, and since then, there's been all kinds of legal battles to get the rights to do this interview, what with everyone wanting to talk to the Messiah. But our network won out."

"Look, I don't know what a network is. Is it some kind of army? And I still don't understand how anyone could have thought I was the prophesied descendant of David."

"Well, you've got good reason to be confused. Once you were dead, rumors started to spread that you rose up alive again. The Romans responded to that by claiming some of your followers stole your body and hid it. Seems they weren't wrong about that. Then your brother James tried to continue your teaching about the Kingdom of God coming at any time, but he was challenged by a man named Paul, who set up a number of communities where his followers believed that you had sacrificed yourself on the cross in order to rid the world of its sins. You were said to have risen up into the sky to join God in Heaven and if people believed you, too, were God, they'd live with you in Paradise forever."

He stared at her for the longest time, dumbfounded. Then he looked down at his wrists. They were scar-free. Nor were there any of the calluses he'd earned working as a *tekton*, a menial laborer, before he'd started preaching. Then he started giggling.

The sound was unnerving to the woman, who stared at him with ever increasing intensity as the giggling became a full-throated laugh that burst out in a roar of coughing and choking as he tried to catch his breath. After a few minutes, he was able to control himself, although it was obvious he was still on the edge of hysterical mirth.

Her next question came in the form of a puzzled expression. Someone handed him a very soft cloth and he wiped his eyes.

"Are they insane; possessed?" he asked.

"Joshua; Jesus, I assure you that millions of people have lived their lives in ways that they believe you wanted them to."

"All I ever wanted was for our people to clean up the Temple and put some pressure on the Romans to ease up on the taxes they were demanding from farmers with small land holdings. I wasn't like one of those Zealots who wanted me to join them in some kind of insane revolt."

"But you did go to Jerusalem during Passover, didn't you?"

"Sure. I figured it would be safe enough with over a hundred people backing me. They were quite willing to cheer me on when I knocked over a few tables and denounced the priests for being Roman collaborators. But did any of them try to protect me when the soldiers came to put me under arrest? Hell, no. They scattered and ran like hyraxes with hyenas on their heels. Especially that Cephas."

The woman looked into one of the boxes. "For those in our

audience who might not recognize the name Cephas," she said, "that's the Aramaic name of the man called Simon Peter. In Greek, it means 'Simon the Rock.'"

Joshua gave an ironic smirk. "When I first saw him, I figured he'd make a good bodyguard—he was big enough—but when the time came, he was the first one bleating, 'Every man for himself!' Rock, my lame, blind ass. He was more like chalk in the end."

"So, you got taken before Pontius Pilate?"

"Pilatus? Where are you getting your information from? The procurator was sleeping, and he certainly wasn't going to be woken up for some small fry like me. That's why I hoped my people would try to free me when that fool of a judge said I should be flogged and marched up to Golgotha. There were only five or six soldiers assigned to the detail, and they wouldn't have been much of a problem if they were outnumbered by a mob. But did anyone even try to put up a fight? Start a bonfire or something to distract them? Don't make me laugh. My so-called loyal followers never once showed their faces; not any of them. Just left me to suffer—and let me tell you, there's no suffering like being nailed to a cross and just left to rot."

"Believe me, Jesus, millions of people understand how horrible a death it must have been."

"Yeah, right. How many of them would have stepped up to defend me? And by the way, stop using Greek. My name is Joshua."

"Okay, Joshua. But I think you'd be surprised at how many Christians today would have stood up for you. Many would have willingly taken your place."

He paused, and his brows knit tightly. "Is it possible? Did my teachings about how we should treat each other as loving neighbors really make a difference? Have men stopped judging and condemning one another? Has God's kingdom come to Earth? To all nations?"

She squirmed a little, and the audience tittered. "Well, not exactly."

"I don't understand."

"Yes, many people try to live like that, but, unfortunately, most aren't too good at it. A lot of things have been done in your name, and you'll be impressed when we show you the cathedrals and the art and you can hear the music—all the stuff that bestows you honor. But," and she held up a cautionary finger, "there are other events that you won't be so happy about. Like wars, and persecutions, and fanatics seeking power over a gullible populace."

"But I never spoke in support of any of those things. If I made the kind of difference you say I did, why hasn't the world gotten better?"

"Because human nature is so complicated. Many of those who claim that they believe you are a part of the 'one true God' think that they ought to do what you say so they won't be punished forever in the burning fires of Hell. Others think you're going to lead an army of angels against the forces of evil and that only those who are on your side will win. That's supposed to happen when all the Jews have converted to Christianity and the great battle of Armageddon takes place."

He shook his head then looked out at the audience.

"Don't any of you get it?" he asked. "Don't you understand? I'm a Jew, and I'm not converting to anything. I'm not and never was a god. I asked that people act justly, that they take care of each other, and that they find ways to put the love of God before everything else."

He tried to see individual faces, but the lights were too bright. His cheeks were wet with tears again, but these came from the sadness his heart was feeling. The audience seemed more restless now, but he tried again to get them to focus on his words.

"It is true that the Kingdom of God is coming; and the day will come when the sons of goodness will do battle with the sons of evil. Where will you be on that day? Repent your sins now, while there is still time."

The woman's voice seemed suddenly amplified as she increased the tempo of her speech.

"Well, ladies and gentlemen, speaking of time, this seems the perfect moment to bring you our specially prepared mini doc, 'The Jesus Legacy,' that explains the rise of Christianity and the impact it has had on world history. For our viewers who might not be well acquainted with how this religion developed over the past two millennia—and particularly for the enlightenment of the most unique and undeniably important guest this show has ever hosted—Jesus, himself—we've prepared a brief, concise summary. Let's have a look."

The lights dimmed and from somewhere above, a kind of glowing window descended through which Joshua could see images that changed magically as a disembodied voice spoke about his life and death and what came after his body was laid in someone's tomb. The next thing he heard was that Magdalene had gone to wash his corpse but found the cave empty and that he supposedly appeared to his bodyguards—a group of twelve men who called themselves Apostles. According to the voice, he told these followers to spread the message that anyone who accepted him as the Messiah would live forever in God's presence. Eventually, those people who accepted that blasphemous teaching were no longer welcome in the synagogues where they first met, and they formed gatherings called churches in their homes. At first there were persecutions, but eventually some emperor made their religion—this Christianity—the official religion of the Empire.

The images flashed rapidly as the story of fights and wars between various Christian groups were conducted for hundreds of years. Fights over whether or not he was a god or, if he were one, at what point in his life did he become divine. Murders and battles were fought over images depicting him in life and death— pictures no Jew would have ever found acceptable and yet all traces of his own Jewish faith erased, even as his people were cursed in his name. Then there were the wars fought against other religions and the slaughters of those who chose one form of this Christianity over another and the burning of individual dissenters who didn't accept what was called orthodox belief.

The voice spoke with pride about colossal temples called cathedrals erected to honor him and his mother, whom (the voice insisted) regularly performed miracles in answer to prayers for her healing interventions. There were artistic expressions carved in stone, painted on walls and ceilings and on canvasses that adorned endless corridors of palaces and buildings called museums. Music, strange and at times seductive in the brief snatches that accompanied the voice, gave praise to God. He found himself horrified as he realized the compelling strains were proclaiming him as the Father's equal.

The pictures of vast multitudes of people gathered in temples or in gigantic courtyards being blessed by the religion's leaders became overwhelming as he heard the explanation that these worshippers believed that the round disc of bread and the cup of wine from which they sipped were actually his own body and blood.

The window went dark as the horror of this last declared abomination swept over him, and he screamed violently.

"Lies! Blasphemy and lies! The temple has become aberrant in God's eyes. I renounce it all!"

For a long moment, the woman visibly shook, and her serene expression was replaced with an open-mouthed gape. Then, in another instant, she recovered and was back in control.

"Jesus—Joshua, this is history. This is what has happened. You have had a major impact on the story of mankind. If you feel that your message has been corrupted, you still have the rest of your life to make the public aware of that. You can still preach, and your words will reach millions of people."

"But the world has accepted falsity and rejected truth. They've done this for over two thousand years. What could I say that would change all that? How long would that take? There isn't enough time in one person's life to bring all of mankind back to the Lord."

Her voice had become calm again.

"But remember, you're Jesus Christ, and that's got to count for a lot. And, speaking about time again, we're just about out of it." She turned to face the audience. "I think Jesus—or should I say, Joshua—has given us much to think about. Certainly, he has made a number of statements that are bound to create a theological dustup of—dare I say it—divine proportions. Will our guest tonight decide to renew his ministry where he left off, or will he develop a whole new career once he has adjusted to the 23rd Century? We hope you'll continue to watch as we bring you news of these ongoing developments. This is Tina Salome signing off and asking you to stay tuned for the upcoming analysis of what Jesus just said, brought to you by the Christian Broadcast Corporation, your greatest hope for salvation in our time."

The lights went off, plunging him into relative darkness. He felt someone undoing the straps that bound him to the cot, and two men helped him put full weight on his legs and guided him forward until he had taken several sure steps. He stood face to face with the woman and gestured toward the now dark window.

"All those things I just saw; I don't understand how this false religion could have anything to do with me."

She shrugged. "Does it matter?"

"Of course it does! You said that this is supposed to be about my life—what I believed; what I tried to teach. But everything's been twisted, and you act like I'm not supposed to care if so many lies are carried out in what you say is my Greek name."

"But, if you know the truth," she reasoned, "why worry about what others think? Besides, your religion is starting to fade."

"I'm a Jew." He was adamant.

"Not to Christians. The god they worship is you." She let out a short laugh. "And your father, Yahweh—"

He gasped and started to pale at the sound of the spoken name again. She chuckled at his expression.

"And the Holy Ghost."

Absolute confusion covered his face. "What on the Lord's earth is that?"

"The third part of your Trinity."

"I accept no other God but God. That is the First Commandment." He looked around the room where he had lain under an almost blinding brightness. "Tell me," he asked, "how many people were here to listen today?"

"You mean in this studio, this room?"

He nodded.

"Oh, maybe about two hundred fifty plus the production crew and technicians. So, around three hundred altogether. But your picture and voice went out to maybe another ten and a half million at least, and by the time the special gets produced, I'd say you'll hit at least two to three billion viewers."

He gasped. "How is that possible?"

"A thing we call technology."

"And could I do the same thing over again?"

"Sure, if you get the right financial backing."

"Then I can tell my real story—teach millions instead of a few dozen at a time."

Her voice was sympathetic, and she purposely made eye contact with him. "Joshua, I doubt you'll ever get the chance to do that."

"But why not?"

"The Christian community isn't going to sit still for anything less than the promise of salvation and a place in Heaven. They'll likely call you a fraud and tune you out."

"But, if they think I'm their messiah, won't they want to hear what I actually preached?"

This time when she laughed, it was full-throated. "You are so naïve, Joshua. If you insist that you are not divine, why would you think they'd want to follow you?" She shook her head. "No, I'm afraid a lot of people have figured it out over the centuries since you died: If they wanted to get the masses to fall in line, they simply had to invoke a resurrected god who was going to send the disobedient to Hell."

"But if that's true, if everything you've been telling me is a mockery of what I lived for, then why did you bring me back in the first place?"

"Why, for money, of course. This production will pay off in the millions."

"Millions of converts?"

"No, of dollars—our equivalent of talents."

He started to open his mouth to respond then paused as the truth caught up with him. He nodded wearily in recognition as a sense of defeat made his limbs feel heavy. "What happens next?" he asked.

"There is a team of doctors and specialists who will be taking you to a secure facility for a complete orientation. Once they've determined you're capable of functioning independently, you'll be able to live normally in this time and place. I suspect that you're going to be a major celebrity for a while more. You might even end up being a rich man."

"That's the last thing I ever wanted to be."

She grinned. "Beats crucifixion, doesn't it?"

He thought about it a moment; thought about what he'd just heard and how his ministry—and his life—had turned out. His shoulders sagged and his breath came in sobs.

"I'm not sure I see the difference," he said. Then his eyes rolled back, and he collapsed into a fetal position.

****

When the paramedics arrived, they found him catatonic.

"BP and respiration are weak. Seems like this guy's in shock. Better get him to the ER stat."

"I'll start an IV." The tech unwrapped the tube and inserted the needle. "You know," he said as he checked the bag, "this seems a little strange. I mean, if this guy really is who they say, why doesn't he just heal himself?"

"Only two possibilities I can think of. One is that he ain't the real article; maybe just a publicity stunt by the CBC or HBO—or both—to boost their ratings."

"What's the other?"

"Maybe all that Bible stuff was just made up like some people have been sayin' all along."

"So, which do you think it is?"

"I could care less. Either way, it won't change my life. I haven't been to church since I was a kid."

"You don't believe in God?"

"Who knows? I sure don't believe in heaven or hell, but I guess I'll find out for sure when I'm dead."

"Maybe. Ever hope they'd bring you back like they did this dude?"

"No way, no thanks. Even if they really could—which I doubt. Sounds too much like a lot of that Christian Broadcasting Corp bullshit to me. Get some guy to play the real Jesus, then after a while they can expose him as a fraud. Make themselves out to be the victims of a deliberate hoax perpetrated by secular scientists who want to discredit the faith of their viewers. Then they can start pledge drives to help fight the atheists who are working to undermine the foundations of religion. Man, I could write the script myself."

"You could be right. But what if? I mean, just maybe— "

"Screw that! Can you imagine what a bitch it would be to have to do your life all over again? All the hassles, the aches and pains, the screw-ups you know you'd make 'cause you hadn't learned any better yet? Nah, once I'm gone, just let me be. No remakes of this piss-poor movie. Too damn hard and too damn pointless for me."

"You're a real cynic, y'know?"

"Yup; but I'm not alone. I saw a thing on the news that said there are twice as many people today who don't go to church than those that do."

"Twice as many? Wow. Makes you feel sorry for this guy if he is who they say. Makes his whole life seem kind of pointless, don't it."

"See what I mean about do-overs? You can have 'em."

"Y'know, it occurs to me that there's something even worse that could happen after you kick off."

"What's that?"

"Eternity. That would have to get boring sooner or later, and there's no escape."

"Amen, brother, amen."

Duality

A personal essay

I remember the day my father, in a fit of rage, locked himself out of the house and onto our porch where he proceeded to smash an oak table into splinters with his fists. But I also remember sitting on that same porch, my sister on one of his knees and I on the other, as the summer rain fell on the flat, tar-paper roof. I can still hear his quiet, deeply resonating voice, like a gently rumbling motor in his chest, as he hugged us close and said, "Listen; just listen to the sound that rain is making. One day, when we're not together, you'll hear that sound again and remember this moment."

I grew up walking the tightrope of my father's extremes, and for most of my life, until he and my mother separated when I was sixteen, I trod cautiously in his presence. He was the fist behind the maternal authority exercised in our family's day-to-day activities. While Dad left for work at five in the morning, nursing one of the dilapidated, hundred-dollar junks he drove thirty miles to his job in the city, Mom was in charge. When he returned, usually after nine o'clock at night, having stayed to hang around and play cards with his friends from "the old neighborhood," he would get a report as to what his children had done during the day. Depending on his mood and our offenses (or lack of them), he would then dispense doses of affection or punishment as my sister and I were in the process of falling asleep. On the occasions when he came home before our bedtimes, we would hug and kiss him, all the while torn between having time during the week with him and hoping that he'd remain affable.

My father spoke fluent belt. For the longest time, the most frightening thing in my world was the sight of him reaching to unbuckle the encircling yard of leather and pulling it from around his waist. It was a form of punishment he had learned from his own father, and it reflected the harsh reality of the way he'd grown up on the mean streets of Depression-era Chicago. My grandfather had emigrated from the southern part of Italy and had found work in the cotton mills of Milwaukee. He married young, and my grandmother bore him three sons. Dad was the second oldest, but when he was still quite young, his big brother died, and his father developed white lung. The family moved to Chicago where there were relatives who might be able to help them out. They didn't—couldn't—and when my dad's mother died during childbirth, Dad and his young brother grew up with only their father's "old country" values. That included taking a beating when they challenged his authority.

Dad once told me how he was trained to accept his father's punishments, beginning from an early age. Whenever he was called into account for a serious transgression—be it public behavior that would reflect poorly on his family or trouble gotten into at school—he was expected to take a standing position, arms at his side, and wait for his own father to deliver the blow to his head. He knew it was coming, but waiting to be struck intensified what was likely a not-too-forceful connection from the older man's hand. This was especially true by the time he was a teenager who was physically larger, stronger, and quicker than his semi-invalid parent. Accordingly, as I grew older, the wild, uncontrolled swings of his belt were replaced by a similar requirement that I, too, had to stand at attention and wait for the smacking I was about to endure.

He was physically powerful, wiry and fast, constantly active, which made him popular with the handful of boys my age who lived on the road where our house stood. He was always ready to play ball, ride bikes, and go on hikes with other kids whose parents allowed them freedom to push the boundaries of exploration because there was an adult with them. The guys would often seek him out on weekends to join in their impromptu activities, and most of the time he would acquiesce and insist that I join in. That I wasn't as physically coordinated as most of the others and lacking the stamina my father exuded, these excursions felt more like a chore than an opportunity to bond with him.

Still, I loved him. He was wise in the ways of the world and often tried to give me advice—kernels of insight that often went over my head or conflicted with the religious instruction I was receiving in my weekly catechism classes.

"Son," he said on more than one occasion, "this world is full of rotten motherfuckers, and I'm the rottenest of them all."

These verbal pearls were usually given out of the hearing of my mother, who detested such language. And while I understood that he was trying to set an example of how manly strength should be expressed, I was always aware they contained nuggets of ironic humor in them.

Once, as we were raking leaves near an open kitchen window, Dad watched me as I huffed and puffed carrying bushels full of damp, rotting materials to a common pile in a nearby field. He paused to make a point.

"Hey, boy, just remember: There are two types of people in this world. Those who work with their heads and those who work with their bodies. The ones who work with their heads are very, very smart. The ones who work with their bodies are assholes."

From the window, my mother's voice sounded a one-word admonishment.

"Nick!"

Dad winced and immediately corrected himself.

"Axles, dear. They're axles."

The silent grins we shared in that moment were part of the bonds of friendship I would eventually come to experience with him as I grew into adulthood. In that vein, I recall a specific incident that helped me realize that he was beginning to recognize my maturing into manhood. He had taken me to work with him one day, and I rode alongside in the cab of his truck as he made local deliveries from Chicago to Gary and back again.

At the end of the workday, he had me accompany him to the dispatcher's office where I sat on a chair while he turned in his paperwork. A half-dozen other men—all truck drivers with hardened, bronze faces—were also crammed in that room, waiting to be cleared for checkout. A moment or two later, another driver came in, scowling as he shuffled his pages, and snapping, "What the fuck—"

Then he saw me sitting there, and realizing whose son I was, shot an embarrassed look at my father and stammered, "Oh, I'm so sorry!"

Dad never batted an eye. Without missing a beat, he pointed to me and said, "It's okay. I've never heard him say 'Shit,' but he probably swears like a bastard."

The room filled with chuckles, and I had a sudden feeling of being accepted by my father's peers. I was still in junior high, but that day I felt grown up. I was acutely aware that my dad was proud of me, that he accepted our differences, but that he also really wanted me to understand his world.

And yet, the fear factor still remained as a divide between us. But the year before he and my mother separated, that barrier was overcome. Not that I believed it at first, but even before he had an inkling that his domestic world would crumble, he made a verbal promise to me that he kept for the rest of our lives.

I had been my usual problem-child self that day. As a high school freshman, I had been sent to the office for making a disturbance in some class I had found boring. Mostly, my offense had involved my continued attempts to carry on conversations with other students, and after my third warning to quiet down, the teacher had kicked me out. This resulted in me drawing three hours of detention, served one at a time after school. When I called my mother to explain the situation, she was very upset as the school was seven miles away, and we only had the one car my father drove to work.

I was still up when Dad got home a bit earlier than usual that evening. He listened to my mother's explanation of the frantic calls she had to make to find a neighbor who would go pick me up. She had been quite upset, needing to be at home for my younger sister, juggling dinner preparations, and coping with her advanced state of pregnancy. This was not something my father wanted to hear, and I could see his face darken with anger.

He raised his voice and began on a diatribe that I knew would result in physical punishment. I started to raise my hands in anticipation of warding off his blows, but he snapped at me to keep my arms down at my sides—as he had had to do for his father. His fingers locked, forming the open hand that could easily floor me with one delivered slap, and I braced for it.

But it didn't come. Instead, I watched his as his shoulders sagged, and a look of compassion came over his face.

"God," he whispered. "You must be scared to death."

Then he was hugging me, squeezing me to him, whispering, "You're too old for me to treat you like this. I swear I won't ever do it again."

And he never did.

Eventually, I graduated and enlisted in the Army. I enjoyed basic training because it was like the obstacle courses my father used to build in our backyard. I could handle infantry training, knowing Dad had gone through it himself and that it was something I knew I could brag to him about when I got home again. I thought I might be sent to 'Nam and face combat like he did during WWII, but Uncle Sam, in his infinite wisdom, sent me to Germany, instilling in me a love of history and providing me with GI Bill money to help me get a college degree.

I had over forty years left with him, and as men, we were close; we were true friends. I understood much of why his life had taken him in the direction it did, and I understood that there was no need to judge him. When he died, in his sleep at the age of eighty-six, it was his live-in girlfriend who called to tell me. Their home was in Tennessee at the time, and when I got there to begin executing his will, she handed me a card he'd been carrying in his wallet for some time. It was for the funeral home with which he had made arrangements for this time. In the upper border, hand-written in the strong lettering that had always been his style, were the words "Call if I'm dead."

I wish I believed in a place from which he could have seen my face at that moment, laughing and crying, and missing the man I would never be able to talk with again. And yet, I still hear his voice, as a deep and resonating memory of my sister and I curled on his lap, whenever summer rains fall on my roof.

About the Author

Tony Marconi is a retired teacher living in Ohio. He has published a book of experimental fiction, *The Complete Works of the Literate Dead*, currently out of print, and several other books, including, *Toscotti's War*; *Upon the Hush of Night*; *Whence Cometh the Dark*; *Until the Stars Are Fallen*; and *On the Nature of Entrenched Prejudice*. He has also written a pamphlet taking on the "clobber verses" in the Bible, *"God vs. Gays: The War that Never Was."* Excerpts can be read on his website, UponMyWord.net.

His poetry has appeared in *The Cornfield Review*, *Grand Little Things*, *Wrath-Bearing Tree*, and *The Voices Project*, and he has had numerous short stories and poems published in various chapbooks and journals.

He loves using the Oxford comma, in part because he learned to include it in his writing when he was younger and is now too old to change his ways. He frequently makes punctuation errors, and his sentences would be too long if it weren't for the keen editorial skills of his amazing wife, Martha Filipic. He owes a great deal of gratitude for her input on output.

He hopes one day to be survived by Martha, his two children, Maggie and Nick, and more than anyone else, his granddaughter, Audrey. And while he has no aspirations for fame and fortune, he would be grateful if, when the time comes, he is remembered fondly by his family, his friends, and his readers.

And yes, he's slipped an Oxford comma into that last sentence, too.

www.ingramcontent.com/pod-product-compliance
Lightning Source LLC
Chambersburg PA
CBHW022017150726
47990CB00002B/693